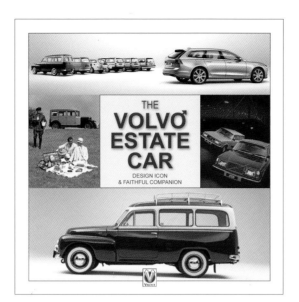

THE VOLVO ESTATE CAR

DESIGN ICON
& FAITHFUL COMPANION

Dedication
To my beautiful little girl, Imogen, who will always be with me.

Some other titles from Veloce Publishing –

Abarth FIAT-based cars (Sparrow)
Alfa Romeo Berlinas (Tipler)
Alfa Romeo Giulia GT & GTA (Tipler)
Alfa Romeo Montreal (Taylor)
Armstrong Siddeley Motors (Smith)
Art Deco and British Car Design (Down)
Bentley MkVI (Nutland)
Bentley Continental, Corniche & Azure 1951-2002 (Bennett)
Bluebird CN7 (Stevens)
BMC Competitions Department Secrets (Browning, Turner, Chambers)
BMW Classic 5 Series 1972 to 2003 (Cranswick)
Book of the Ducati 750 SS 'round-case' 1974 (Falloon)
Book of the Ferrari 288 GTO (Sackey, Materazzi)
Book of the Ford Thunderbird from 1954 (Long)
Book of the Jaguar XJ-S (Long)
Book of the Lamborghini Urraco (Landsem)
book of the Mazda MX-5 Miata (Long)
Book of the Porsche 356 (Long)
Book of the Standard Motor Company (Robson)
Book of the Volkswagen Type 3 (Glen)
Britains Toy Models Catalogues 1970-1979 (Pullen)
BRM – A mechanic's tale (Salmon)
Bugatti – The 8-cylinder Touring Cars 1920-34 (Price, Arbey)
Bugatti 57 – The Last French Bugatti (Price)
Bugatti Type 40 (Price, Arbey)
Bugatti Type 46 & 50 (Price)
Bugatti Type 57 Grand Prix (Tomlinson)
Car-tastrophes (John, Fowler)
Chrysler 300 (Ackerson)
Chrysler 300 Series – Pedigree, Power and Performance since 1955 (Ackerson)
Chrysler PT Cruiser (Ackerson)
Cortina (Robson)

Cosworth – The Search For Power (6th Edn) (Robson)
Daimler SP250 (Long)
Darracq Called Genevieve (Laredo)
Datsun Fairlady Roadster to 280ZX – The Z-car Story (Long)
Datsun Fairlady Roadster to 280ZX – The Z-car Story (Long)
Dino (Long)
Dodge Dynamite! (Grist)
Dune Buggy Files (Hale)
Dune Buggy Handbook (Hale)
East German Motor Vehicles in Pictures (Suhr, Weinreich)
Fate of the Sleeping Beauties (op de Weegh)
Fiat & Abarth 124 Spider & Coupé (Tipler)
Fiat & Abarth 500 & 600 (Bobbitt)
Fiat & Abarth 500, 600 & Seicento (Bobbitt)
Ford F-100/F-150 Pickup 1953 to 1996 (Ackerson)
Ford F-150 Pickup 1997-2005 (Ackerson)
Ford in Miniature (Olson)
Ford Midsize Muscle – Fairlane, Torino & Ranchero (Cranswick)
Ford Models Y & C (Roberts)
GM in Miniature (Olson)
Great Small Fiats (Ward)
GT (Dawson)
How to Draw & Paint Cars (Gardiner)
How to illustrate and design Concept Cars (Dewey)
Inside the Rolls-Royce & Bentley Styling Department 1971 to 2001 (Hull)
Intermeccanica – The Story of the Prancing Bull (McCredie, Reisner)
Jaguar – All the Cars (4th Edn) (Thorley)
Jaguar MkI & II Saloons (Sparrow)
Jaguar XJ220 – The Inside Story (Moreton)
Jeep CJ 1945 – 1986 (Ackerson)
Jeep Wrangler from 1987 (Ackerson)
Jowett Jupiter – The car that leaped to fame (Nankivell)

Karmann Ghia Coupé & Cabriolet (Bobbitt)
La Carrera Panamericana (Tipler)
Lea-Francis Story (Price)
Making a Morgan (Hensing)
Mazda MX-5 Miata (Long)
Mazda Mx-5 Miata Roadster (Long)
Mazda Rotary-engined Cars (Cranswick)
Mercedes G-Wagen (Long)
Mercedes-Benz SL (Long)
Mercedes-Benz SLK (Long)
Mercedes-Benz W123 series (Long)
MGA (Price Williams)
Micro Trucks (Mort)
Microcars at large! (Quellin)
Mini Minor to Asia Minor (West)
Mitsubishi Lancer Evo (Long)
Morgan 3 Wheeler (Dron)
Morris Minor (Newell)
Motor Movies – The Posters! (Veysey)
Motorhomes – The Illustrated History (Jenkinson)
Nissan 300zx/350z The Z Car Story (Long)
Nissan GT-R Supercar: Born to race (Gorodji)
Pass – your theory and practical driving tests (Gibson, Hoole)
Peking to Paris (Young)
Plastic Toy Cars of the 1950s & 1960s (Ralston)
Pocket Guide to Britains Farm Model & Toy Tractors 1998-2008 (Pullen)
Pocket Guide to Britains Farm Model Balers & Combines 1967-2007 (Pullen)
Porsche (Meredith)
Porsche – The Racing 914s (Smith)
Porsche 908 (Födisch, Neßhöver, Roßbach, Schwarz)
Porsche 911 (Long)
Porsche 911 Carrera – The Last of the Evolution (Corlett)
Porsche 914 & 914-6 (Long)
Porsche 914 & 914-6 (Long)
Porsche 924 (Long)

Porsche 924 Carreras (Smith)
Porsche 928 (Long)
Porsche Boxster (Long)
Preston Tucker & Others (Linde)
RAC Rally Action! (Gardiner)
Rise of Jaguar (Price)
Rolls-Royce Silver Shadow/Bentley T-Series, Camargue & Corniche (Bobbitt)
Rolls-Royce Silver Spirit & Silver Spur, Bentley Mulsanne, Eight, Continental, Brooklands & Azure (Bobbitt)
Rootes Cars of the 1950s, 1960s & 1970s – Hillman, Humber, Singer, Sunbeam & Talbot (Rowe)
Rover P4 (Bobbitt)
Russian Motor Vehicles (Kelly)
RX-7 Mazda's Rotary Engine Sports Car (Long)
Singer Story (Atkinson)
Sleeping Beauties USA (Marek)
Steve Hole's Kit Car Cornucopia (Hole)
Subaru Impreza (Long)
Tatra – The Legacy of Hans Ledwinka (Margolius, Henry)
This Day in Automotive History (Corey)
To Boldly Go – twenty six vehicle designs that dared to be different (Hull)
Toyota Celica & Supra (Long)
Triumph & Standard Cars 1945 to 1984 (Warrington)
Triumph TR6 (Kimberley)
Unraced ... (Collins)
Volkswagen Beetle Cabriolet (Bobbitt)
Volkswagen Bus Book (Bobbitt)
Volvo Estate (Hollebone)
VW Beetle (Copping)
VW Golf (Copping, Cservenka)
Wonderful Wacky World of Marketingmobiles (Hale)
You & Your Jaguar XK/XKR (Thorley)

www.veloce.co.uk

First published in July 2017 by Veloce Publishing Limited, Veloce House, Parkway Farm Business Park, Middle Farm Way, Poundbury, Dorchester DT1 3AR, England. Fax 01305 250479 / e-mail info@veloce.co.uk / web www.veloce.co.uk or www.velocebooks.com. ISBN: 978-1-787110-75-5 UPC: 6-36847-01075-1

THE
VOLVO♂
ESTATE
CAR

DESIGN ICON
& FAITHFUL COMPANION

VELOCE

Contents

Introduction

The Volvo estate car has become a household name, recognised globally as the definitive estate car, and yet, it is in some ways also an unsung hero of the automotive world, less-celebrated in book form than many of its contemporaries. This book hopes to redress the balance.

It traces the development of this best-known of all estate cars from its origins, descended from early 20th century motorised wagons and brakes, to its most recent incarnation in the second decade of the 21st century, and beyond.

In old-fashioned parlance, a 'wagon' was a four-wheeled, horse-drawn vehicle, for passenger or cargo use. One of its many roles was to transport hunting parties or picnickers to the countryside. The term 'brake' may also be traced back to the horse-drawn carriage, a brake being a rudimentary wagon used for breaking in young horses to harness-work, while a 'shooting-brake' was a vehicle used to carry shooting parties with their equipment and game. Here, we see these two early vehicles converge to become the estate car.

Note that I have used the automotive term 'estate' throughout the book, rather than the American terms 'station wagon' or just 'wagon,' to refer to a vehicle with a roof that extends rearward, and an opening rear door to allow access to a glazed cargo area.

Volvo was not the first company to build this type of car, but it made it its own. The Volvo estate became – and has remained – the vehicle of choice for families and tradespeople. For many owners and their children, the Volvo estate is not simply a car – it became an integral part of their childhood – an adopted member of the family, that took them on trips to the seaside, holidays, and the daily school run.

By the 1970s, the Volvo name had become synonymous with the family estate car. Despite numerous attempts to steal its crown, the many times award-winning Volvo estate car has remained the firm favourite of millions.

Love it or hate it, a Volvo estate is more than just a car. From the first Volvo car to its latest offerings, the company's emphasis has been on safety, durability, and a responsible attitude to the world around, and the Volvo estate deservedly became such a family favourite for pretty much anyone who could afford one. It is for this reason, and my personal love of this car, that I wanted to write this book – and I have been given a wonderful selection of images with which to illustrate it.

Ashley Hollebone
West Sussex

Acknowledgements

I would like to express my gratitude to Per-Åke Fröberg of Volvo Cars Heritage in Sweden for the assistance given to me, and to Lars Gerdin at the Volvo Heritage archives, for the time spent going through the photographic archives. Volvo has been warm and welcoming from the outset. Many images within this book have never been published before, and it is thanks to Volvo for preserving its wonderful archives that I have had the chance to chronicle the heritage of its most worthy car.

The early days of Volvo

The Volvo company was founded in 1927 in Gothenburg in Sweden, 'Volvo' being the Latin word for 'I roll' – an appropriate and memorable name for a car company.

Europe was just emerging from the fraught days that had followed the First World War, and the world was becoming motorcar crazy.

Before the war, only a small percentage of the population owned cars – railways carried people to their destinations, which were limited to where the railway network stretched – that was, of course, if your country even had one! At the outbreak of WW1, motorcars were still very expensive.

The 1920s saw a significant expansion in motor manufacturing, and the public began to enjoy the freedoms the motorcar offered. It was not the large, expensive makes that were advancing; more the cheaper models, often made by manufacturers that had been in business as blacksmiths and bicycle makers. There were many weird and wonderful contraptions offered during this period, but it was far more than just an experimental age: some of these traditional craftsmen and companies would limp into the next decade, while others would return to their more primitive roots. This is my favourite era in our motoring heritage, due to the huge variety of makes and models offered.

However, no one rivalled Henry Ford's company for mass production and popularity: Since its introduction in 1908, Ford's Model T had dominated car sales – in

1918 more than half the cars in the USA were Model Ts – but by the mid-20s, sales were flagging, and in 1927 Ford brought out a new model, Ford Model A.

Furthermore, it was not just in countries like the United States, France and Great Britain that car sales were on the up. Sweden, too, had room to produce its own home-grown vehicles. But starting from nothing and launching a brand new motorcar brand from scratch is no easy task, especially if you plan on taking on rivals such as Ford!

The Volvo company was founded by two brilliant young men, each with a vision of the kind of cars they wanted to create. The first was Assar Gabrielsson, an economist with a background in government. He began working for the SKF bearing company (Svenska Kullagerfabriken) in 1916. Four years later, he become managing director of the French side of the business, an important post that would get his mind ticking.

At this time, France was a hotbed for light car design and manufacture. The proud nation had, after all, staged the first ever motor races, which helped the development of famous French manufacturers, not just of the motorcars themselves, but also of vital component suppliers. For most of Europe, these charming small cars sold well, but for Sweden's rugged and challenging climate, they had limited appeal.

By 1923, Gabrielsson was sales manager for the entire SKF company. During his time at SKF, he became acquainted with Design Engineer Gustaf

Larson. In August 1924, the two men found time to meet over a Crayfish lunch, bursting with enthusiasm to discuss their ideas of taking the firm into motorcar production. Whilst it was a business meeting, it was also one of passion for the subject, and this meeting was one of the most important steps in the history of the Volvo brand. Both men were in agreement that Sweden should produce its own car, rather than relying on imported American brands, which, while tending to be larger and more durable than European cars, still offered little concession to the Scandinavian climate and terrain. Both men agreed that they could take the bearing company to new horizons; after all, it was already supplying the automotive industry. Furthermore – and perhaps most significantly – both believed that quality and safety were of paramount importance, a concept that still applies to Volvo cars today.

One year after the crayfish lunch meeting, the new Swedish car company was ready to begin manufacturing its first production vehicles. Gabrielsson and Larson had strict criteria for their design so that it would cope with the cold climate and harsh roads. These new cars had to be very solid, so they wouldn't shake themselves apart on the unforgiving roads of Scandinavia. They had to endure freezing winter months, and be safe all year round. This remains the benchmark for Volvo cars today. There are not many other motor manufacturers that have stayed true to their founding ethos. Rolls-Royce is one, continually aspiring to make 'The Best Car in the World,' and, whilst I am not comparing the product, the brands share the same exacting standards.

The rest is history, as some may say. The first Volvo model was named ÖV4 (open vehicle, four-seater). It's launch came with a slight technical hitch: the first car off the production line reversed back into the factory instead of driving out of it – the differential gear in the rear axle had been fitted incorrectly, and first gear had

Volvo name and logo
The name Volvo first appeared in 1911 as a trademark for SKF, although it was shelved until 1915, when a separate division was set up with the intention to produce a new type of bearing.
The logo was taken from the ancient chemical symbol for iron, denoting strength; a characteristic to which the car has held firm throughout the brand's history.

ASSAR GABRIELSSON

The Volvo Company founders.

GUSTAF LARSON

SKF bearing with the first trademark Volvo name stamped on it. Volvo means 'I roll' in Latin.

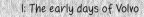

Gothenburg factory
plan showing a
similar layout of ÖV4
production to that
of the Model T.

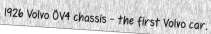

1926 Volvo ÖV4 chassis – the first Volvo car.

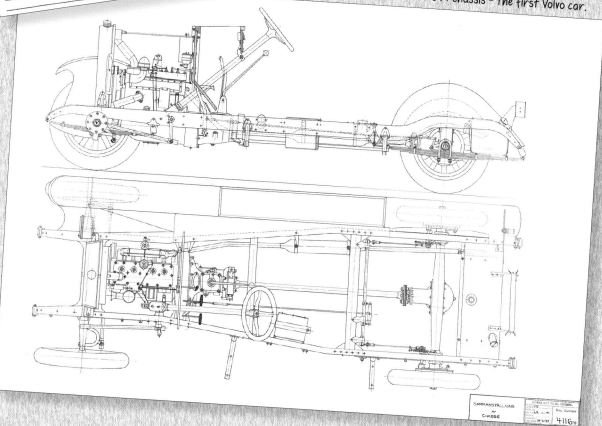

SAMMANSTÄLLNING
AV
CHASSIE

Reg Nummer
4116

become reverse. This set the official introduction day for the ÖV4 back by one day, to 14 April 1927.

The open-seater ÖV4 was in keeping with the period, and similar in appearance to contemporary American machines. Somewhat strange, one might think, that Volvo's first car would be an open touring car rather than a saloon, given that it was specially made for motoring in cold climates; yet, of 275 ÖV4s produced, only 70 were saloons – a reflection of the era of vintage motoring. Towards the end of the decade, Volvo launched new models, and was even offering commercial variants based upon its car chassis, with the first six-cylinder Volvo car going on sale in 1929.

continued on page 15

The first Volvo car chassis awaits marriage to new coachwork.

The first car rolled off the line on April 14, 1927 and so the Volvo car company began.

1926 prototype ÖV4: note the absence of a Volvo badge and disc wheels.

The same car, revealing its well-trimmed interior.

Drivers had little choice but to test their vehicles in harsh winter conditions.

A simple way to demonstrate the centre of gravity.

Another prototype: progressive for the period, Volvo consistently featured female drivers in its adverts.

The ÖV4 was a true family car, capable of performing many roles. This is one of the ten pre-series prototype cars manufactured in Stockholm.

An early advertisement: the car the nation had been waiting for. Note the reference to Volvo Limited in Gothenburg, now a separate entity from SKF bearings.

'The Swedish Car' – an early advertisement for the ÖV4.

In 1928 the first saloon entered production (PV4). The seats could be laid flat to make two beds.

A newly-finished PV4 fabric saloon outside the factory. Four wheel brakes a new option.

Around 200 touring bodies were scrapped in favour of the saloon. Here, traditional Weymann-style coachbuilding is under way.

VOLVO

During the first year of car production, Volvo had made advances with its car – and reduced the price to boost sales.

An early handbook for the PV4 with lovely artwork.

A number of ÖV4 touring car bodies were converted into light pick-ups for the telephone exchange.

1927 Volvo ÖV4 pick-up.

The first ever Volvo estate car: this specially ordered PV4 had a rear tailgate for loading carrying cases.

In April 1929, Volvo brought out a new model, the six-cylinder PV651, to replace the ÖV4, though it had only been in production for two years. Volvo had quickly realised that there was scope for a larger car. Its success was to help the company become independent (it had been a subsidiary of SKF), and to purchase its own factory.

One of the biggest sectors for Volvo was for taxis, and the PV651 was targeted at that market. However, its appeal was universal. In 1929, 1383 cars were produced. Of that number, 27 examples only were exported, proving loyal local demand. A year later, Volvo produced a slightly larger version: the PV652 with seven seats. Does that seat number sound familiar? These large vintage and post-vintage saloons had a striking visual similarity to their American rivals and would not have looked out of place on Fifth Avenue. Over time, this 600 series model would undergo various refinements, but its basic chassis and running gear would soldier on in production, until a radical change in design occurred.

As Volvo entered a new decade, it would quickly adapt to the increasing demand for its cars, while changes in fashion meant that the previous models now appeared quite dated. Within just ten years, the motor car had become more of a stylish status symbol than solely a way in which to shuttle from A to B. If the 1920s gave people a reason to find hope after the atrocities of war, the 1930s became a party.

Boxy shapes were becoming a thing of the past: Art Deco's flowing curves and sweeping lines were everywhere. It was a time of experimentation, too. Volvo now had a wide range of vehicles available: taxis, vans and saloons, and even very attractive drophead coupés. This wonderful selection had arrived in a very short space of time, given the company was not even ten years old.

With the Swedish public, Volvo now found itself as popular for its commercial variants as for its cars. During this period, there were numerous coachbuilders supplying versatile vans and pick-ups.

This was the most progressive decade of car design so far; the motorcar had become part of a new culture, offering freedom and adventure for all. The design of

In April 1929 PV4 production was replaced by the six-cylinder PV651; Volvo targeted the taxi market.

Artwork for lubrication specifications booklet on the PV651.

The Volvo estate car – design icon and faithful companion

The first Volvo police van.

Swedish motorists had been used to American imports. The six-cylinder Volvo would form the backbone of the company for many years.

An impressive fleet of new PV65ls await the Swedish police force, which would grow very fond of Volvo.

Based on the same chassis, this 1926 PV657 ambulance was well suited to the task.

just about any object from teapots to steam trains was influenced by the streamlining and ultra-modern style of the period. The Czechoslovakian Tatra 77 of 1934 was a radical example of aerodynamic Art Deco modernism; and Chrysler, in the US, launched a car simply called the

The new 1936 PV51 had a limited run of stylish drophead coupés and highlights. There was much diversity within the Volvo platform in the early days, including taxis, commercials, and saloons.

17

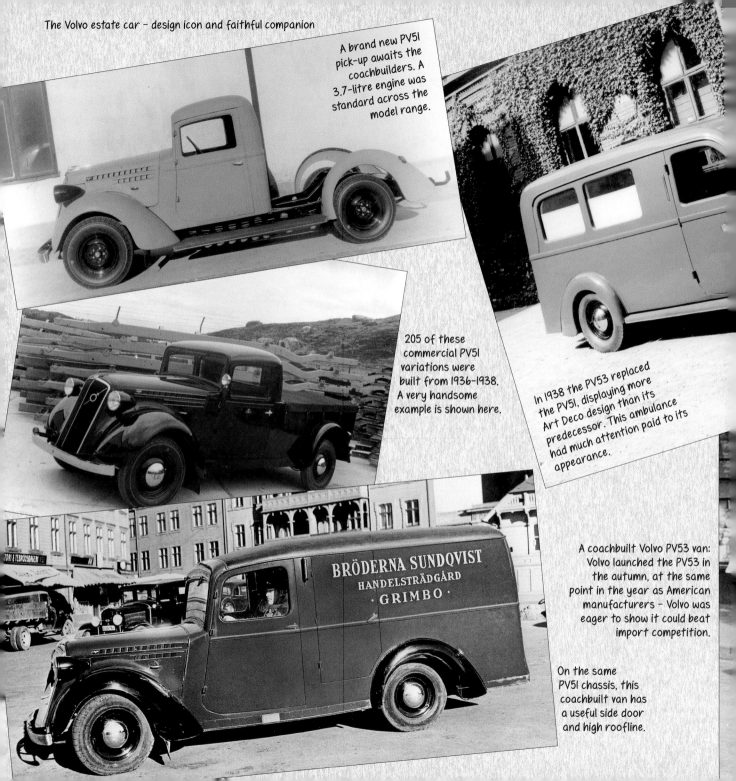

A brand new PV51 pick-up awaits the coachbuilders. A 3.7-litre engine was standard across the model range.

205 of these commercial PV51 variations were built from 1936–1938. A very handsome example is shown here.

In 1938 the PV53 replaced the PV51, displaying more Art Deco design than its predecessor. This ambulance had much attention paid to its appearance.

BRÖDERNA SUNDQVIST
HANDELSTRÄDGÅRD
· GRIMBO ·

A coachbuilt Volvo PV53 van: Volvo launched the PV53 in the autumn, at the same point in the year as American manufacturers – Volvo was eager to show it could beat import competition.

On the same PV51 chassis, this coachbuilt van has a useful side door and high roofline.

PV53 ambulance.

ORSTADIUS BOKTRYCKERI A.-B.

FÄRGER

Volvo supplied the chassis cabs, painted black as standard. This van's newly completed coachwork is ready for paint. Few of these early examples have survived.

With its high roofline and customised cargo area, this model is quite different from the one pictured above.

This PV53 from Stockholm has been customised for transporting window awnings to its customers.

1930s Art Deco influenced the futuristic Tatra 77.

TATRA "77" LA VOITURE ÉLÉGANTE

The 1934 Chrysler Airflow – similar in design to the PV36, and too radical for the American public. (Courtesy Hemmings Daily)

'Airflow,' which incorporated elements of aircraft design.

Unfortunately, and somewhat surprisingly, the Chrysler Airflow is rare today – not only because of its age, but mainly because of its slow sales. As beautiful as it was, it was just too far ahead of its time; many felt its styling was too extreme, and motorists were not inclined to abandon their more conservative models. It would seem that injecting the world with Art Deco did little to transform the everyday.

Launched in April 1936, Volvo's latest model, the PV36, looked remarkably similar to the Chrysler Airflow. This was the first truly modern Volvo, embracing contemporary influences in design head on. However, this did not become the commercial success that it should have been. Such a shame that only 500 of these aerodynamic cars were produced.

The following year another new Volvo model was introduced, the less-flamboyant PV51. Whilst it shared the same engine and running gear as its lavish counterpart, this car was cheaper, and, as result, sold very well. Its robust body coped well with mistreatment – Volvo even rolled one to test its strength.

Despite all this innovation in car design, at the time Volvo was still primarily a commercial vehicle manufacturer, selling twice as many commercial vehicles as cars.

On 1 September 1939, Germany invaded Poland, and Europe was at war.

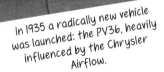

In 1935 a radically new vehicle was launched: the PV36, heavily influenced by the Chrysler Airflow.

Just 500 of these PV36 cars were made. Like the Chrysler Airflow, the PV36 failed to win over the public.

21

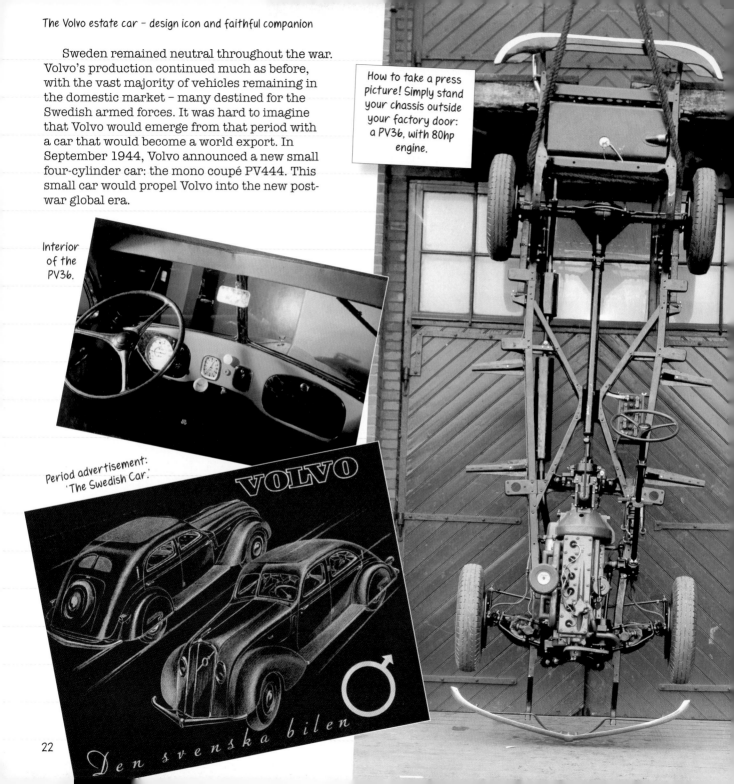

Sweden remained neutral throughout the war. Volvo's production continued much as before, with the vast majority of vehicles remaining in the domestic market – many destined for the Swedish armed forces. It was hard to imagine that Volvo would emerge from that period with a car that would become a world export. In September 1944, Volvo announced a new small four-cylinder car: the mono coupé PV444. This small car would propel Volvo into the new post-war global era.

How to take a press picture! Simply stand your chassis outside your factory door: a PV36, with 80hp engine.

Interior of the PV36.

Period advertisement: 'The Swedish Car.'

VOLVO

Den svenska bilen

Outside the factory:
the V-styled
bumper subtly
suggests Volvo.

The romance of the era and the
motorcar: both of which were soon
to be shaken up.

2 Duett

Volvo has been making trucks and light commercial vehicles almost as long as it has passenger cars. The first commercial vehicle produced (in 1928) was called the LV4, LV denoting Lastvagn (truck) and although it utilised the same running gear as the ÖV4 passenger car, the truck variant had a stronger chassis. There is a wonderfully restored LV45 bus on display at the Volvo Museum in Gothenburg. However, ÖV4 chassis were also available for lighter commercial duties.

During the Second World War, manufacturing had focused on military vehicles and munitions, and few civilian vehicles were produced. Once peace was

A 1928 LV4 truck at the Volvo Museum; an important step towards the development of a versatile domestic vehicle.

In 1944, Volvo launched the new PV444. Everything about the PV444 was new.

restored, the public craved new cars. With fuel rationing, and materials still in short supply, Volvo saw the need for a smaller vehicle: its new car, the PV444, with a 1400cc engine, entered production in 1947, and achieved strong sales: Volvo had got it right. This new car offered not just Sweden, but also the US, what was needed: a small durable and economical saloon car with modern styling and ease of use; and it was strong! This became the benchmark for future Volvos.

The Volvo PV444 became extremely popular. It became the small passenger car of choice in Sweden and beyond. Its size, strength and durability meant that it *should* have been popular with coachbuilders, too. However, the PV444 was of unitary construction, with no separate chassis, and coachbuilders needed a separate chassis to customise into small commercial vehicles, such as vans and pick-up trucks.

In 1949, a new prototype was devised. In all but the frame and its cross-members, it shared the PV444's components. The chassis was supported by leaf springs, and weighed 725kg with a body-dependent payload of

The beautiful green interior of this PV444 A series car marks Volvo's move into the post-war period.

The PV444 A: most examples were black; the one in this publicity picture was intended for the United States market.

500-550kg – although, as any Volvo owner will tell you, the cars are capable of being overloaded to a degree, without much concern.

The new car-derived van was called the PV445, and it quickly became the vehicle of choice for both small businesses and larger corporate mainstream fleets. At the time, Sweden had around 70 coachbuilders, many now busy crafting various bodies on the first 500 PV455 chassis.

1952 advertisement for a coachbuilt PV445 delivery van.

The pick-up was one of the most durable versions of the PV445. The chassis were supplied to coachbuilders ready-to-drive.

There was nothing particularly radical or new about Volvo's offering – lots of motor manufacturers had been producing customised commercial vehicles, using the chassis of Model T Fords, Austin Sevens and other cars. However, the Volvo was Sweden's very own car, and a source of patriotic pride. It proved versatile, with many vans converted into passenger-carrying vehicles by the addition of a rear bench seat and side windows, often doubling up as a trade vehicle during the week, and family car at weekends for lakeside picnics and camping trips. Perhaps this was the American influence starting to show, but one thing was certain: it was the beginning of a new trend. People were adapting an existing vehicle to fit their needs. Now Volvo had to look at the PV445 once again, with this in mind.

Period advertisement clearly aimed at the local tradesperson – the salesman points out the attractive little PV445 van.

The new PV445 chassis quickly gained a good reputation and had strong orders from coachbuilders, but in 1952 Volvo found itself with a surplus, perhaps partly due to their simple and quick construction. There was growing competition, too: other European manufacturers had started to produce their own light vans, constructing the coachwork in-house rather than using coachbuilders (a trade that was on the wane); and PV445 cars were of such sturdy quality that they simply did not need to be replaced, which is great for the owner, but not so great for the manufacturer trying to sell new ones. In early 1952, Assar Gabrielsson noted that there were around 1500 unsold units dominating the factory grounds. He decided that Volvo should build its own van.

The engineer put in charge of the project was Erik Skoog. He had been involved with the development of the PV444 car back in 1943. He quickly saw the 445 chassis' potential, and drafted a series of drawings. Coachbuilders had already been building vans, and some station wagon vehicles on the chassis, but it was Skoog who would lay the foundation for the first true Volvo estate. He and his team designed a versatile body for the 445 chassis, suitable for transporting either goods or people. On May 2nd 1952, Skoog presented his model and drawings to Gabrielsson, and was given the go-ahead to start work on developing the car. Six months later, a full scale wooden mock-up had been produced.

In the autumn of 1950, a new taxi model of the 800 series was presented, the PV831 and 834. Commercial chassis were still sold to coachbuilders, as this 1950 model demonstrates.

The large PV832 coachbuilt station wagon provided a taste of things to come.

4 July 1953

A separate heading because it is one of the most significant dates in the history of the Volvo estate. Founding partner of Volvo, Gabrielsson proudly took delivery of the very first car that rolled off the line as an estate version, registered as a light truck, and given the type variant of 445DH. The construction method was quite complex compared to previous models, and initial production was rather slow to get off the ground, as tooling and production lines became standardised. The first van

The first Volvo-produced van, this prototype was based on the PV444.

In-house production of Volvo vans started in 1953, distinguishable from coachbuilt examples by their double rear doors and flush side panels.

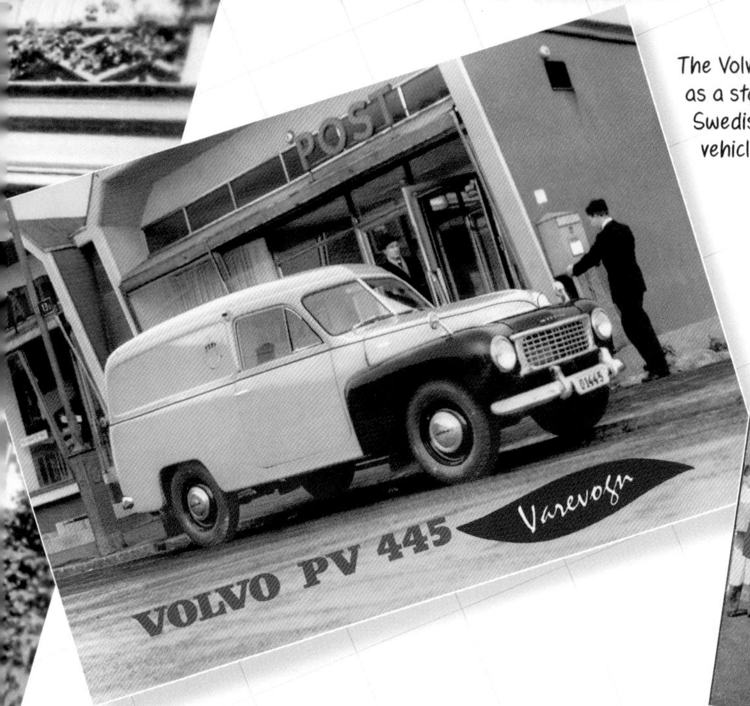
POST
VOLVO PV 445
Varevogn

The Volvo-built PV445 van, which, from 1953, was available as a station wagon and van from the showroom: the Swedish postal service became a great fan of Volvo vehicles.

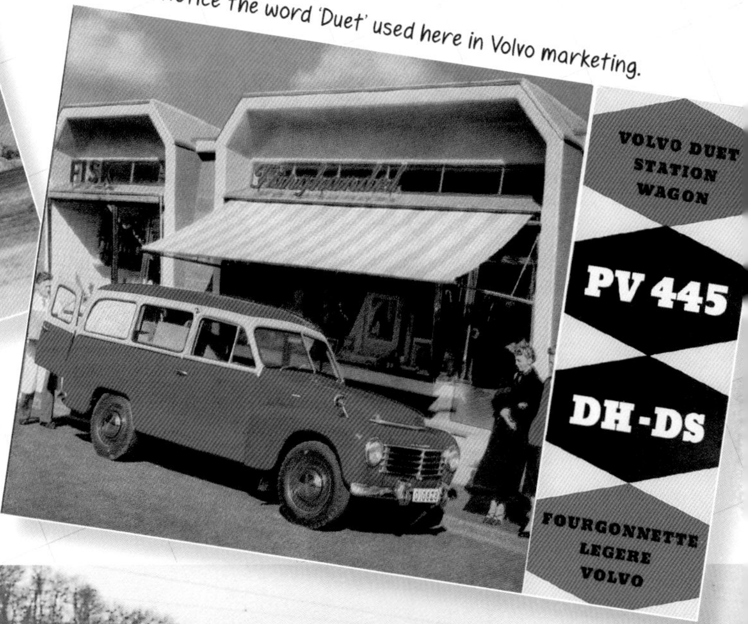
FISK
VOLVO DUET
STATION
WAGON
PV 445
DH-DS
FOURGONNETTE
LEGERE
VOLVO

Notice the word 'Duet' used here in Volvo marketing.

Volvo press picture for the first series of PV445 vans.

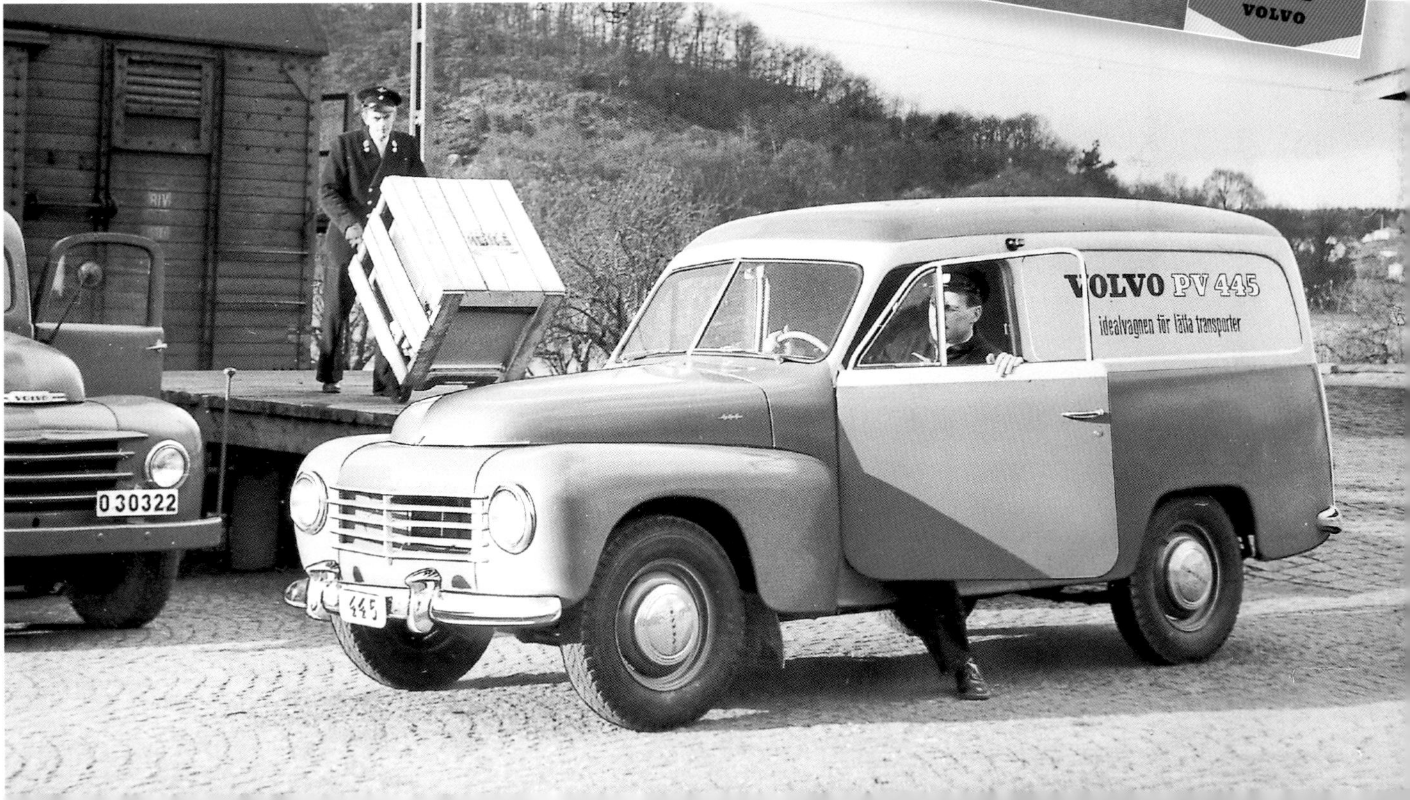
VOLVO PV 445
idealvagnen för lätta transporter
O 30322
445

version was completed on 20 November, and designated the 445 DS.

It was an instant success – at the time, there was probably not another car in existence as practical as this new Volvo model. Despite its relatively small size, it could swallow up an extraordinary amount of luggage, largely due to the generous height of its cargo area. It became known as the 'Duett' (later, the 'Duet' in the US), from its dual role as a work vehicle during the week and a family car at weekends.

The Duett looked similar to some of the coachbuilt examples, but was differentiated by its smooth body sides, while coachbuilt types had rear wings as part of their lines, with a slightly deeper front roof line. The Duett had a rigid pressed steel and welded body, much like that of its sister PV444 car, whereas the coachbuilt examples were usually made using traditional pre war techniques, with an ash frame to which the metal panels are attached. The latter was less practical in the long term, as each element causes the other to deteriorate over time under damp conditions.

The Duett featured tall rear doors, and, due to the load capacity it offered, it became very popular with a variety of commercial customers, including television and radio suppliers, tradesmen, and even the police. During the 1950s and '60s, the Duett would have been a common sight throughout Sweden, with plenty of examples in service with nationalised departments, such as telecoms and power services.

Despite high domestic sales, Volvo realised that there was not sufficient custom in Sweden to sustain production, and Gabrielsson began to look for ways to conquer the American market. Volvo had been exporting there since the 1930s, its cars appealing to the American outdoor lifestyle, but it had not yet made a significant impact.

Gabrielsson visited America in 1954,

The first Duett station wagon offered by Volvo, in 1953.

Early Duett estate car.

Volvo Duett – sjudagarsbilen

A period Duett advertisement.

VOLVO P 445

ARKIVEXEMPLAR
Exportreklamavdelningen

A period van advertisement.

whilst the firm was secretly working away on the next generation model, which we will come to in the next chapter. With Volvo's successor of the Duett's sister car, designated the PV554, the outlook for greater dominance seemed promising: it had 'US market' written all over it. Meanwhile, Volvo was developing an updated version of the Duett.

In the summer of 1955, Volvo brought out this new version of the estate: the 445 PH. The key difference from its predecessors was that this model was aimed directly at the family car market. It also included higher trim levels than the van upon which it was based. Then, in 1957, an important optional extra was made for the Duett that would transform the car into a seven seater – an extra row of seats in the rear cargo area.

continued on page 34

VOLVO Duett

bilen som är två

A period Duett advertisement.

The 1957 PV445 series received a new front grille, B16 engine, and a four-speed gearbox.

The Volvo estate car – design icon and faithful companion

A period Duett advertisement.

VOLVO P 445 AMBULANCE

Model voor inrichting en uitrusting

AB VOLVO

An unusual coachbuilt Volvo ambulance, featuring an extended wheel base and an extra rear door.

The versatile Duett could be used for work during the week, and for family adventures at the weekend.

The seat belt

Swedish engineer, Nils Bohlin joined Volvo in 1958 to work on the development of a safety feature that he had invented. Bohlin's creation was an adaptation of a primitive lap belt most often used in racing cars. The original offered little protection and was not taken up by any motor manufacturer. With a background at Saab in aircraft ejector seat design, Bohlin had valuable knowledge on securing bodies to seats when subject to sudden force. His invention was the three point harness – the seat belt, as we know it today. Volvo had quickly realised its potential to save lives, and commissioned Bohlin to develop it. Whilst the seat belt has evolved to include pre-tensioners and other more advanced systems, the basic design has remained the same as it was when Volvo launched it to the world in 1959, and fitted front seat belts as standard across its entire range.

Volvo was the first manufacturer to give its customers the seat belt – and it gifted them to the world, too. This is perhaps its greatest contribution ever to automobile safety: it could have earned hundreds of millions of dollars from this invention, but instead gave it away free, so that other manufacturers would be encouraged to fit seat belts and thus save lives. Without question, Volvo achieved its objective. It is very hard to think of a major corporation doing such a selfless and upstanding act today, and Volvo should be highly commended for it. According to Volvo, by the time Nils Bohlin died in September 2002, his invention had saved more than one million lives over the 40 years of its existence. The Volvo name has always been associated with safety, and this part of its story demonstrates that like nothing else.

Typical of the time, most Duetts were finished in two-tone paint.

The cargo area had wooden panelling and a well-designed floor: practical and stylish.

1956 Duett: this example is part of the Volvo heritage collection. Although the Duett started life as a commercial vehicle, it wasn't out of place among saloon cars.

This beautifully restored example exudes the spirit of adventure.

By autumn 1960, the Duett name was changed to 210, signifying a new updated version. It had been subtly modernised, as far as the design would allow. The 1940s-style split screen and 1950s two-tone paintwork had now been superseded by one pastel colour. A four-speed gearbox was also introduced – a much-welcomed addition, bringing the car up-to-date and offering far more refinement as roads became faster. Seat belts were now a standard fitting on the Duett and other vehicles throughout the range.

Increasing demand for the 210 ensured its place as a favourite workhorse during the '60s. In May 1962, the 210 received the new B18 engine, an engine that would pave the way for the next generation of Volvo cars. The B18 engine had a reputation for being almost indestructible, and, even as examples grew older, would continue to perform reliably, often despite some neglect.

Ten years after its initial launch, the Duett/210 had strong orders – it had become a very capable vehicle for the expanding world. It's quite a typical Volvo tale that products brought out to replace the aging 210 seemed to have little effect on its popularity. The Amazon estate was introduced in 1962, and its replacement, the 145, in 1967, but the 210 soldiered on until it was finally withdrawn from production in 1969. By then, the car was becoming outdated.

Volvo models traditionally last longer in production than many of their rivals because the company gets it right first time. Its loyal customers enjoy long-term ownership, with a car that becomes part of the family.

The very last Duett rolled off the production line in February 1969 and straight into the Volvo Museum collection in Gothenburg, where it can be seen today. Over its 16-year production life, the Duett/210 remained a much-loved Swedish favourite, and was

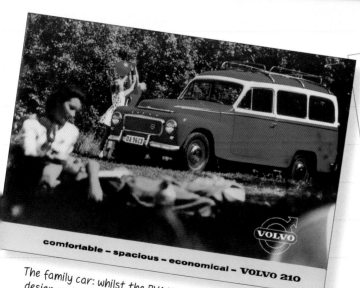

comfortable – spacious – economical – **VOLVO 210**

The family car: whilst the PV445 was influenced by American design and culture, it was perfect for the Swedish lifestyle.

VOLVO 210 *Duett*
bilen för arbete och fritid

A car for work and leisure: the new generation Duett became the 210, now a single colour, and with a one-piece windscreen.

The Volvo estate car – design icon and faithful companion

the foundation for the Volvo estate car as we know it today.

Volvo Duett/210 Production 1955-1969: 101,492.

Volvo 210 van – the vehicle of choice for telephone engineers.

VOLVO 210

ARKIVEXEMPLAR
Kundinformationsavdelningen

FÄRG

Volvo 210 tilbyr större lastevolum til lavere kostnad enn noen annen bil av samme type og klasse. ■ Volvo tilbyr en kombinasjon av økonomiske fordeler. Særdeles høy 2. hånds verdi, velkjent slitestyrke og rikelig standard- med bl.a. fabrikkmonterte 3-punks sikkerhetsbelter. ■ Lett å laste.

VOLVO 210 skåpvagn

For renodlat transportbruk
bygger Volvo även en skåpvagnsmodell av Duett.
Skåpvagnen har inte baksäte, vilket gör
att lastutrymmet blir något större än hos
Duetten – över tre kubikmeter.

TELE

What better vehicle for on-site maintenance for Volvo trucks?

SERVICE

36

3 Amazon

In 1956, Volvo announced a new car: the Amazon (initially the Amason, and designated the 121 and 122S abroad). Its name was inspired by the female warriors of Greek myth, and it was to become one of the most iconic of all Volvo's cars. The Amazon was launched at the beginning of September 1956, in the Swedish town of Örebro, and it was clear at first sight that this car marked the beginning of a new era for Volvo. The styling was modern, with two oval air intakes at the front. The rear wings were extended and ended with a hint of a fin.

Designed by Jan Wilsgaard, Chief Designer at Volvo, its stylish look, reminiscent of a scaled-down Buick, was clearly influenced by America, but it also drew inspiration from contemporary Italian and British design. It was also the first Volvo to be offered in right-hand drive for British, South African and Australian markets. The 1956 Amazon showcased the company's ethos and design and was the first Volvo to conquer the global market.

The Amazon 121/122 S also saw the introduction of some innovative safety features, such as a padded dashboard, laminated windscreen, and seat belt

At its launch in 1956, the Volvo Amazon had two-tone paint, and a very American look.

As these photos of the early mock-up show, many of the concept's features were retained. However, it looked more like a Chevy Nomad.

It wasn't long before Volvo developed a totally new estate car.

attachment points for both front and rear seats – a sign of things to come from Volvo.

The new Volvo also saw the introduction of ergonomic seats – another world first. These were developed in consultation with medical experts, and consisted of thick cushions of polyester foam. This foam was carefully shaped, and was firmer at the edges for extra support when cornering.

A sporty two-door version of the Amazon was brought out at the New York Motor Show in April 1959. Twin carburettors, a sports steering wheel and rev counter set it apart from the standard saloon.

In early 1961, Volvo started work developing a new estate car version of the Amazon, the 220, intended to replace the 210/Duett. The first prototype looked similar to the American Chevy Nomad, featuring a split tailgate, and fins.

As is the fate of many prototypes, a watered-down production model eventually appeared before the press at the 1962 Stockholm motor show. The world finally got to see the new Volvo estate car. Designed as a family station wagon, it had a greater level of comfort than its Duett predecessor. It came with more efficient load capacity thanks to its flat floor, too, although it weighed 10kg less than the 210/Duett. One of the most welcome features on the new estate car was its two-piece drop-down tailgate, retained from the prototype – ideal for using as a seat, sheltered by the upper roof-hinged door, when parked, and perfect for carrying longer-than-normal loads, such as ladders, surfboards, and timber. Colourwise, if you bought an

continued on page 42

The new 220 estate car offered greater loading capacity than the Duett, without compromising the refinement and performance of the Amazon saloon.

Duett 210 and Amazon: both models were offered, until 210 production stopped in 1969, by which time it was quite outdated.

Volvo was keen to advertise the fact that it was the first car manufacturer to offer seat belts, as standard, with the Amazon.

US brochure cover for the 122S (Sport), which featured twin SU carburettors with 100bhp.

Famous Volvo owners
General Colin Powell, has at times owned up to six old Volvos, and was presented with an Amazon estate by Bill Clinton and Al Gore when he retired as chairman of the Joint Chiefs in 1993. (*New York Times*)

Fittingly, a Swedish Amazon estate police car.

A Volvo estate through-and-through: its lines can still be seen on the very latest of the Volvo range today.

Amazon estate car in 1962, it could be any colour you like – so long as it was Mist Green!

Personally, I feel that the Amazon looks much better as an estate than a saloon. It has clean, elegant proportions, and comes complete with a design feature that has endured to this day: Volvo estates have a definite 'look' which can be traced back to the Amazon estate

Amazon estates are quite a rare sight today, partly because they were put to hard work, but also due to a blight that affected many cars of the period: rust. In many cases, after decades of use, the still-sturdy engine would practically run away from the crumbling bodywork. It's not that the Amazon estate rusted more than other vehicles, just that it was often subjected

— en symbol för hög svensk kvalitet och teknik

The Volvo range of 1964.

The split tailgate was one of the most useful features on the Amazon estate.

A Gothenburg press picture: the professional's choice.

to a whole lot more abuse, because of the trust people placed in its toughness.

Who was buying the new Volvo estate? Volvo gained a new customer base with this car, one that would bring it loyal supporters for many decades to come. The estate car was becoming fashionable, popular for its practicality and for its style. It became the car of choice for media types, photographers and other such professionals. Adverts promoted it as part of an aspirational lifestyle, with images of affluent families at play, and it became a status symbol in its own right.

Sales and feedback told their own story: the Amazon 220 was a resounding success. It was also the first Volvo to feature a folding rear seat, creating a load length of 183cm. Volvo advertising even suggested sleeping in the Amazon, and Volvo produced its own woollen blankets for the job.

A twin carburettor version was offered for the more enthusiastic driver.

During this period, the increase in production began to overwhelm the Torslanda plant at Gothenburg. With its sights on North America, Volvo chose to open a new facility overseas. The location chosen was Halifax, Nova Scotia, Canada, the closest port to Gothenburg for the Atlantic crossing. Cars would be assembled from semi-component form at the Halifax plant. This saved on resources at Gothenburg and had greater cost

220 Swedish brochure cover.

The sporty 123GT was launched in 1966. The Amazon was the first right-hand drive Volvo to be offered in the UK, from 1958.

Fastest car in Britain
Guy Martin, TV presenter and racing driver, has a 1967 Vöx estate – a super-charged version of the Amazon, which Martin says he reckons is the fastest car in Britain.
(Sunday Times)

Interior of the 123GT, showing the rev counter, and unique three-spoke steering wheel.

The B18B engine of a 123GT – the same engine as used in the P1800 sports car.

From 1967 Volvo fitted a collapsible steering column in the Amazon, among other new safety features. That same year, Volvo presented the world's first rear-facing child seat.

savings at the other end. There was now no need to transport brand new cars thousands of miles across the ocean, exposing them to the corrosive sea air of the North Atlantic, and increasing potential corrosion before they even make it to dealers' showrooms. This was, later, an issue with the Jensen-produced P1800 sports car, unpainted examples of which were corroded badly by the sea voyage between England and Sweden until Volvo took control of production in-house (see Chapter 5).

In 1969, the Amazon 220's engine was updated with the new 1986cc B20 version, which now gave 82hp in standard form. This engine would power Volvo estate car models until 1981. However, time moves on, and a replacement for the Amazon estate was on the way: the last Amazon estate car rolled off the line in 1969.

As with the Duett before it, the Amazon estate was a much-loved car – it was not in production for as long, as technology and fashion was evolving quickly, and Volvo

had a more advanced car in the pipeline, but it was an important step away from coachbuilt van production, and towards producing a dedicated family estate car.

During its production run, the 220 attracted a strong customer following for Volvo, so strong that it was to tailor its new model to suit this new customer base. The Amazon played an important part in Volvo's emergence as the leading marque for estate cars. Volvo knew that the replacement would have a lot to live up to.

Amazon 220 Estate Production 1962-1969: 73,197.

Production ended in 1969, but many of these cars soldiered on for years. Despite neglect in many cases, the cars kept going until rust defeated them.

4 145

The Volvo 144 saloon car was launched in August 1966, to an audience of almost 400 journalists at Gothenberg, with simultaneous unveilings in Oslo, Helsinki, and Copenhagen.

With the 140 series, Volvo's management, under CEO Gunnar Engellau, introduced a tri-digit system for naming its cars in which the first digit indicated the model series, the second digit the number of cylinders, and the third the number of doors. It also planned several different chassis versions from the outset: a departure from previous practice. The new car was larger than the Amazon, but in the same weight and price bracket, and with the same wheelbase as its predecessors, the PV 544 and the Amazon. It was intended to carry four or five people in comfort, and there was a strong emphasis on safety.

The new 140 series was to be a consumer delight. Disc brakes on both axles and seat belts were, of course, standard, along with equipment that included front head rests. The model numbers were quite simple to identify: 142 two-door, 144 four-door and, later, the 145 five-door. The new 145 estate car began production in 1968. Work had actually begun on the 140 series back in June 1960, when the Duett was still selling well, and the Amazon estate hadn't even made it as far as prototype stage, such was Volvo's forward thinking and future planning. On 27 November 1967, the first concept model of the 145 estate car was displayed. This would define the shape of what was to become the most famous Volvo estate car of all time: the 245/240 estate (see Chapter 6).

The 1967 Volvo 145.

VOLVO 145

An early UK sales brochure for the 145.

Imagine all the advantages of the 140 series in an Estate Car.

Carpets now replaced rubber flooring on the 140 series. However, it was the cavernous loading capacity that would eclipse the competition.

Open the enormous tailgate.
This is how a really spacious Estate Car should be!

"Open the enormous tailgate. This is how a really spacious Estate Car should be!" – a quote from the 1969 UK sales brochure for the 145.

It was no exaggeration, either. With the rear seat folded flat, the load space seemed vast. Another Volvo first was its revolutionary braking system. Dual circuit brakes were a standard feature on the 140 series. This meant that, if the car developed a brake fault, only two wheels would lose braking. Safe brakes on the 140 and later 240 series cars are

The spare wheel is easily accessible and does not infringe upon the cargo area. It's hidden behind an attractive form pressing.

The cargo area is cosily upholstered and easily looked after thanks to the hard wearing textile materials. Totally free from unnecessary details. Rich in practical features.
The rear seat backrest is quickly and easily folded down. From either the right or left-hand sides. The Volvo 145 has now a smooth, wide and 74" (188 cm) long cargo carrying floor.
By lifting two textile-clad flaps in the car floor a well protected cavity storage space of approximately 3.5 cu.ft. capacity is revealed. Excellent for valuables or fragile goods. This cavity space can also be utilized for the fitting of an extra seat — available as an accessory.

Early 145s had chrome grilles, split rear side windows, and push button door handles.

The sumptuous interior of the 145, and modern straight dashboard layout, took the car into a league of its own.

a brilliant asset. Sadly, the 145 is a rare car today, and often absent from car events.

The Duett had been a popular choice for owners of small businesses, so what would fill that void? In 1969, the 145 was joined by a more commercial variant, the 145 express. At first sight, you would be forgiven for mistaking it for an ambulance – and it *was* used for that purpose: in essence, it was a case of van meets luxury car. Its raised roof line and small cab-mounted roof rack offered greater loading capacity than the Duett. The interior was decked out with wooden rails and a bulkhead behind the front seats. Production ended in 1974 for both the 145 and the 145 express. Just 7000 of the latter were built; another very rare sight today.

Heavy-duty rear suspension ensured that the 145 would be able to take whatever

The boxy Volvo estate car shape would last for over two decades.

was thrown at it. Initially the B18 powered the 145, as with the saloon variant, but, from the Autumn of 1969, the new B20 engine was used. This was a bored-out 2.0-litre version of the B18. Three-speed automatic transmission was available on the 90hp model, while the 118hp engine came with twin carburettors, and was rightly called the 145S (Sport). The large 145

was surprisingly light and agile to drive – the first real luxury Volvo to offer mile-munching comfort, something that would soon spread across the rest of the Volvo range.

The seven-seat option had proved popular with customers, and the design of the 145 had a seven-seat version from the beginning; this time without any

VOLVO 144/145

Polisbil

4-dörrars Volvo 144 och herrgårdsvagnen Volvo 145 för polisbruk. Spe cialutrustade enligt Svenska Rikspolisstyrelsens riktlinjer. Konstruerac för att tåla stora påfrestningar under krävande körförhållanden.

The Swedish police 140 cars: their highly impressive turning radius of just 21ft almost put London taxis to shame.

The Volvo 145 had 71cu ft capacity with the rear seats folded flush to the floor. A folding child seat option was added, transforming the 145 into a seven-seater.

Bakluckan lyfts automatiskt med två kraftiga gasfjädrar.

Under lastrummets golv finns ett lätt åtkomligt extra utrymme för t.ex. ömtåligt bagage.

Reservhjulet har fått en diskret och praktisk stående placering bakom vänster bakhjul.

Swedish sales brochure, showing off the attractive space of the 145.

The Volvo surpassed any rivals with its superior build, quality and ride. The 145 is my favourite estate car model.

For the tradesman, demanding even more space, the 145 Express was launched in 1969, and featured a raised roof line.

compromise over the vehicle's loading capabilities. A clever rear-facing seat, which could be neatly folded and concealed in a recessed floor, meant that full use could be made of the generous interior.

With the folding seat raised, its storage cavity became a footwell for the child passengers. For cars without the optional child seat, that extra space provided very useful storage.

In 1975, the 145 featured in a new British BBC sitcom: *The Good Life*, set in middle class suburbia. The Volvo estate car had become shorthand for the aspirational middle class, and was thus the perfect car for Jerry and Margot Leadbetter, the snobbish 'couple next door.'

145 Production 1967-1974: 268,317.

VOLVO 145 Express

Volvo 145 Express — en ny variant i 140-serien avsedd för varutransport. Finns i två versioner — en med plåtklädda sidor och en med glasrutor runt om. Glasversionen kan även erhållas med baksäte.

Swedish 145 Express sales brochure: available as a van without seats, or as a conventional estate car, the Express was popular with tradesman and taxi drivers.

VOLVO 145 EXPRESS
4 coches en uno

Volvo 145 Express en versión especial para cuatro misiones distintas: taxi, transporte, escolar y ambulancia. Seguro, económico y ágil. Un vehículo de avanzada técnica.

A smart looking Express taxi.

This standard 145 taxi would have been more than capable of accommodating the whole family's luggage.

A 145 Express ambulance with an extended front roof line. Very few Express cars have survived today.

1970 revisions: most notable, the flush door handles, plastic grille with the Volvo diagonal line, one-piece rear side windows, and front indicators placed on the wings.

VOLVO 145 FAMILIARE

By 1973, there were bulbous front indicator lenses, and an enhanced Volvo badge centred in the grille. The bumpers were higher to meet American safety standards.

A crash-pad steering wheel, and a centre console with a switch layout, that would remain largely unchanged for the next twenty years.

Whilst the 145 would undergo various changes, the rear end remained the same.

A 1973 145.

Fitted with the B20E engine, and Bosch K Jetronic fuel-injection system, the 145 had reached its peak.

In 1974 the 145 received large energy-sapping bumpers, in order to meet American safety regulations.

Opposite: The 145 set the standard for a new generation, and was an iconic design from Volvo. The Volvo estate was set to become a legend.

VOLVO 145 de Luxe
FUEL INJECTION

Elegant, Leistungsstark, Sicher.

Als exklusive Variante der normalen Kombiwagen bietet der Volvo 145 de Luxe Fuel Injection bei-spielhaften Ausstattungs- und Platzkomfort. Tem-peramentvoller Einspritz-

motor mit 115 PS. Drei ansprechende Metallic-Lacke zur Auswahl: Gold-Metallic, Grünblau-Metal-lic und Hellblau-Metallic. Selbstverständlich besitzt auch dieses Modell die

umfangreiche Volvo-Sicherheitsausrüstung, die kräftigen Stoßstangen und die H4-Halogenscheinwer-fer. Die Geräumigkeit ist selbst bei einem Wagen dieser Klasse überraschend groß.

Unser sportlichster Fünftürer.

Der Motor im Volvo 145 de Luxe Fuel Injection ist kein hochgezüchteter Rennwagenmotor, er er-möglicht aber trotzdem eine ausgesprochen sportliche Fahrweise. Aus 2 dm³ Hubraum

entnehmen wir volle 115 DIN-PS, und das bei einer Verdichtung von nur 8,7:1. Für die große Leistung sorgt die neue Saugrohr-Benzinein-spritzung. Sie ist auber-ordentlich funktions-sicher und wartungs-freundlich. Automati-sches Dreistufen-Getrie-

be auf Wunsch. Fünf Personen haben be-quem Platz. Trotzdem ist noch viel Raum für Gepäck und sperrige Ge-genstände vorhanden. Bei heruntergeklapptem Rücksitz stehen fast 2.000 dm³ Laderaum zur Verfügung.

Lernen Sie diesen Volvo näher kennen. Am be-sten auf einer Probefahrt. Er verdient es.

VOLVO
AB VOLVO GÖTEBORG SCHWEDEN

A German sales brochure: the 145 de Luxe was the top-of-the-range 145 estate car.

5 P1800 ES

In the early 1960s, when television producers of the hit UK series *The Saint* were searching for a new car in which to place the lead character (played by Roger Moore), they asked Jaguar for an E-Type or two. Jaguar turned them down, so they looked at other options and turned to Volvo, which saw the potential for some good 'free' advertising. The car chosen was the new P1800, which

oozed charisma, and the coupé became one of the most famous cars to feature in a television series: today many refer to the P1800 as 'The Saint's Car' – one of the best examples of product placement.

But what of the P1800, a clever cocktail of well-proven standard Volvo components, housed within a casing of automotive glamour and Scandinavian durability? Whilst the dashboard may have looked like a '50s rocket ship, the rest of the car was quite utilitarian. Initially the cars were built by British sports car maker, Jensen, in England, due to lack of capacity at Volvo's plant in Sweden. However, after delays in production, and rust issues with the bodyshells, due to their exposure to corrosive sea air during transport, Volvo would soon take charge of the build itself.

For many people, the P1800 is the most beautiful of all Volvo's models. Prior to the P1800, Volvo had not been known for its sports cars. (There was the Volvo Sport of 1959, but only 64 were ever produced, and production halted before the car had a decent chance to be marketed, due to third-party quality issues). In contrast, the P1800 was a popular car; it sold well, and demonstrated how the brand could showcase its very best qualities. In 1972, a new variant would emerge that featured the best of both branches of Volvo cars: half sports, half estate. The ES was conceived as a shooting brake, a

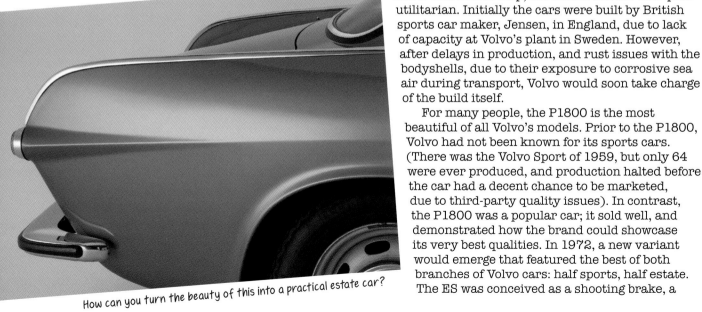

How can you turn the beauty of this into a practical estate car?

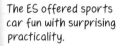

The ES offered sports car fun with surprising practicality.

sort of practical sports car. It was never going to compete with its bigger brother in the 145 range, and, with more interior space than the coupé, and a price tag £400 higher, the ES appealed to a different type of customer. The all-glass tailgate helped rear visibility and cut down on weight, and was an aesthetically pleasing design – well received, especially in the important US market, where journalists praised the car's practicality, and loved its elegant tailgate.

The world was becoming increasingly safety conscious, America especially, and new safety and emissions legislation was being introduced there. Many European cars had to be heavily modified to meet America's strict import rules; the MGB, for example, lost its shiny chrome

The large glass tailgate helped with visibility. Four wheel disc brakes were standard in 1969 on all cars.

bumpers, replaced by ugly black rubber; and power-sapping emissions control pipework was introduced. Volvo was not immune from this: in the last days of the 145, a new big bumper was introduced, to meet US safety requirements – but what of the P1800?

The ES was discontinued gracefully, with its beauty still intact, in June 1973, one year after than the coupé had ceased production. Just 8077 P1800ES cars had been built. It may have had the shortest production run for a Volvo estate, but it helped prolong the life of the P1800 sports car, and to demonstrate Volvo's capabilities. The next generation of small Dutch-built Volvo cars – the 480 models – however, were to be something of a let-down, but that's a story for a different book.

P1800 ES Production 1972-1973: 8078.

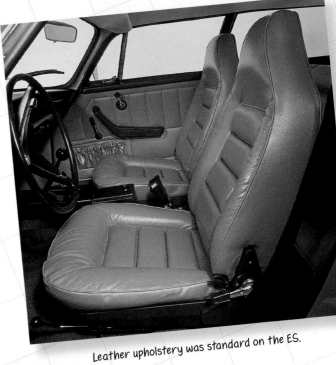

Leather upholstery was standard on the ES.

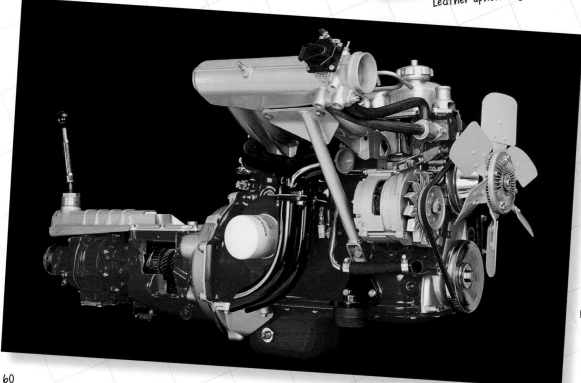

B20F fuel-injected engine of the ES with just 112bhp. Despite having more weight, the ES had less power.

Some say that the ES is a better-looking car than the final coupé version.

Irv Gordon with his 3,000,000-mile-busting P1800.

Volvo durability

At 4pm on 18 September 2013, Irvin 'Irv' Gordon (USA) clocked up his three-millionth mile in his 1966 Volvo 1800S while driving near the village of Girdwood, south of Anchorage in Alaska, USA. By 1 May 2014, he had driven 3,039,122 miles. (Guinness World Records)

6 245 | 265 | 240

In April 1972 at the Geneva Motor Show, Volvo unveiled to the world its new concept car: the VESC (Volvo Experimental Safety Car). Years ahead of its time in terms of safety design, it featured crumple zones, a 'disappearing steering wheel' which pulled away from the driver in a frontal collision, rollover protection, anti-lock braking system, automatic seat belts, airbags, pop-up head restraints, interior trim, and reversing sensors – even headlamp washers and wipers. The VESC attracted enormous attention worldwide. Many of its safety features were to find their way into the next Volvo estate car: the 245.

A lot of thought had gone into the VESC – in fact, it is fair to say that the VESC project was more of a limited production run than a one-off concept car. Multiple examples were produced, all variations on a theme. Thankfully, a few of these cars have been

The first 245 UK sales brochure.

The 245 was designed by Jan Wilsgaard, Volvo's Chief Designer from 1950 until 1990, who had also designed the P1800ES and 140 series.

The most revolutionary new element of the Volvo estate car was its engine: the overhead camshaft B2I and B2IE fuel-injection.

preserved, and at least one of them is on display at the Volvo Museum in Gothenburg.

This period of increasingly strict safety legislation worldwide influenced the shape of vehicles of many different brands, and saw the death of the all-American muscle car: rising oil prices and the addition of power-sapping emission control systems put an end to the dream of the high octane Mopar.

With the launch of the Volvo 240 and 260 Series in autumn 1974, the Volvo estate became a celebrity in its own right. The new car was the culmination of years of Volvo safety and engineering development – and was firmly focused on maintaining customer reassurance and trust. Volvo had always placed strong emphasis on safety, and legislation was moving in the same direction, led by America: now was Volvo's time. The 240 series was to become Volvo's most enduring ever, with close to 2.9 million cars rolling off the production line over a 19-year period. Volvo had earned a formidable reputation for safety throughout the world. Indeed, the US government used the Volvo 240 saloon as its reference point for car safety, and it was to set the standard for both safety and environmental responsibility through the 1970s and 1980s.

Designed by Jan Wilsgaard, the 240 was initially available with eight variations (242L, 242DL, 244DL, 244GL, 245L, 245DL, 264DL and 264GL). At first

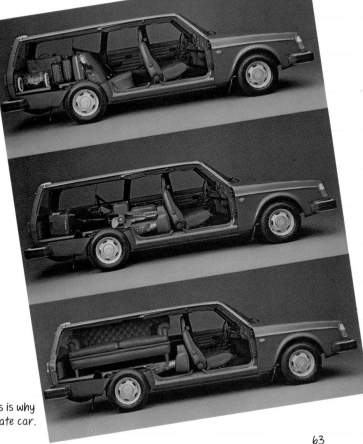

What can you get in yours? This is why customers love the classic Volvo estate car.

The round headlamps of the DL.

The leading line: whilst the 245 GLE was a powerful car, an even more upmarket model was offered, with a new V6 engine.

GLE interiors were very luxurious: you could be forgiven for forgetting that this was an estate car.

glance, the new car looked like the earlier 140/160 series: it shared the same bodyshell and was largely the same in appearance from the cowl rearward, but the 240 was far from just being a revised 140. It was also heavily influenced by the VESC.

The MacPherson strut-type front suspension was new, while the rear was a modified version of that in the 140. The bumpers and front grille of the 240 were completely restyled – the most obvious visual departure from earlier cars. The 245's big bumpers blended well into the design of the car.

Structurally, the 245 was built around a cage, hidden by the interior trim. Side impact bars were incorporated within the doors, while huge body crumple zones in the front and rear ensured that the overall safety of the driver and passengers was greatly improved in the event of a crash.

Compared to the 145, the interior of the 245 was far more comfortable. The dashboard layout was revised, with updated plastics, hard-wearing seats, and a new range of switch gear, while thanks to the rack and pinion steering, the 245 was a joy to drive. The driving position offered a commanding view of the road, and the car had an impressive turning radius of 32ft.

The biggest change was to the engine: it had a capacity of 2127cc with outputs of

Golf clubs and shooting parties: Volvo's marketing made clear that the 245 GLE and 265 were cars of distinction.

97hp for the B21A carburettor version and 123hp for the B21E injection version, and Volvo's new luxury estate, the 265, used a completely new V6 90-degree engine – the result of collaboration between Volvo and French car manufacturers, Renault and Peugeot, and hence known as the PRV. (The first of these engines were officially introduced on 3 October 1974 in the Volvo 264.). The engine had a capacity of 2127cc with outputs of 97hp for the B21A carburettor version, and 123hp for the B21E injection version. The B27E

continued on page 70

A 245 DL publicity shot.

Volvo 245

Two versions of the 245 are available—the 245 DL and the 245 GLE. They have identical dimensions and carrying capacities. The 245 DL has a very comprehensive specification but the GLE offers that 'something extra' for the individual who wants higher performance and an even more luxurious specification.

The DL, GL and GLE were easily identified by their headlamps.

A UK sales brochure.

The nose of the 245 had to be raised slightly to fit the V6 engine under the bonnet. Chrome door handle surrounds also identify the car as a GLE 245.

Italian coachbuilder Bertone, more used to Lamborghini than cold climate cars, was brought in to create a stylish coupé: the 262C used the V6 engine.

Metallic green was the chosen launch colour for the 265 in the UK.

Volvo estate cars in film and on TV

If you want to portray an academic, a solidly middle class family, or an antique dealer, the car that fits the bill is a Volvo estate: in *Beetlejuice*, Geena Davis and Alec Baldwin are driving a 245 when they plunge to their deaths to avoid hitting a dog, Lovejoy, the antique dealer in the TV series of the same name, drove a 265.

A US-spec 265, with its twin-headlamp conversion.

The Volvo estate car

VOLVO
245/265

VOLVO
245

UK sales brochure artwork.

Endorsed by Ikea
Ikea founder, Ingvar
Kamprad, drove a
240 GL for two decades,
and only gave it up in
his late 80s. Famously
parsimonious, he was
once refused entry
to a business awards
ceremony because he
arrived on the bus.

DLs being sprayed in the Torslanda
area of the Gothenburg factory.
Later, that name would be used for
a special edition 240.

Research data from the VESC concept car led to numerous safety features being incorporated in the 240 series.

had a capacity of 2664cc, giving 140hp and brought the Volvo range in line with offerings from other premium manufacturers such as Mercedes-Benz. Quite adequate for such a car, although more power is always welcome and this was to be addressed in the next decade. The base level DL had 100hp in 1977, while the 245 continued to be tweaked over the years.

The overhead camshaft B19-B21 engine was installed at a slant angle of 15 degrees, similar to some other cars of the period, such as the Lotus Elite. This made room for the new range of fuel-injection systems on these engines. The Volvo estate was increasingly adapting to the faster pace of life each decade brought. Volvo was now competing with premium brands, in Germany and, of course, North American. The plan was to push the Volvo estate right up into the luxury league.

The 265 had power steering and air-conditioning, and its V6 gave plenty of torque for towing – ideal for family camping holidays. Its automatic variant used the Borg Warner automatic gearbox, typical for other high-end cars, too, such as Jaguar. This is a long-lasting unit that rarely encounters issues, reinforcing Volvo's reputation for reliability. On the downside was higher fuel consumption.

Although designed in the early '70s, the V6 lasted well into the next decade and successfully elevated Volvo to the luxury car category. Any owner of a V6 Volvo will be aware of its faults: head gasket failures, high fuel consumption, and so on, but it was a major factor in turning the Volvo estate into a familiar sight on many a manor house gravel drive.

Today, diesel cars are commonplace, but back in the 1970s, they were not. Diesel engines of the time were unrefined, underpowered, dirty, and noisy. In 1978, Volvo teamed up with Volkswagen to supply a brand new six-cylinder diesel engine, and this became available in the 245, designated the D6. It was showcased at the Paris Motorshow of that year. This engine was exclusively used by Volvo, while the VW group utilised the five- and four-cylinder versions for vehicles in its range, from the LT van to Audi saloons. In the 245, there were two main options: the 2.4-litre D24 and the 2.0-litre D20 – both very good motors, as long as you were in no hurry! The D6 had a claimed output of a mere 82hp at 4800rpm, which would have

been noticeably lower than the petrol versions. The car was not available in the UK, but proved popular in Europe and North America. However, US emissions standards dampened its sales in North America, and California rejected it entirely. The 245 was Volvo's first diesel-powered estate car; a pioneer in that sense, at least.

Thanks to the way the cars were built, with zinc-coated steel and air cleverly ducted through the sills, the 245 lasted extremely well. Plastic wheelarch liners helped prevent unwanted build-up of salt, mud, and corrosive matter to preserve the car for the future. It may not be a sexy car to look at, but it was one of the most practical things on the road. The clever placement of the tailgate hinges on top of the roof, too, ensured not only that the tailgate would open wider, but it kept a flush aperture for loading.

In 1979, the four-millionth Volvo car rolled off the Torslanda production line: a 245 DL, and in 1980, the 244GLT (Grand Luxe Touring) model was introduced, with a four-cylinder B23E injection engine, and with the V6 141hp engine in the estate version.

240

We have now reached the very pinnacle of the tale of the world's most iconic estate car. A 245 DL entered the world record book in 1980, when Garry Sowerby and Ken Langley circumnavigated the world in 74 days. The faithful 'Brick' as it became known, entered a new decade and took a leap forward: enter the age of turbo power!

A 2.3-litre B23E engine was announced in 1980, which was a boarded-out B21 with 140hp. One of the first models to use this new engine carried a new name, the GLT (Grand Lux Touring) and was to be the sporty offering of the range. The car was very striking to look at, with black trim instead of chrome along the window surrounds and bumper, five-spoke alloy wheels with low profile tyres, and

Volvo V6 engine
The same V6 engine used in the 265 was to feature in the DMC DeLorean sports car that powered Marty McFly to 1955 and back again in the 1985 film, Back to the Future and its sequels.

The 245 Transfer was a cross between a minibus and an executive estate car taxi.

In 1980 this 245DL entered the world record books, when Gary Sowerby and Ken Langley circumnavigated the world in 74 days.

leather or plush interior. It was not intended for the UK market, but some 200 were reportedly sold there: most of the UK GLTs had a black leather interior.

In 1981, the 245 had a major face-lift. In some examples, the B21 engine were married to Garrett T3 turbochargers. This was named the B21FT in the US market and the B21E within other markets. If the 240 had garnered criticism for being a sluggish tank, the turbo had arrived to change that conception: in standard form, its output was 157hp. (US cars didn't perform quite so well, due to their emissions systems.) At its launch, and for some time after, the 240 Turbo was one the world's fastest estate cars. As with the diesel

Thankfully, the hearse is quite rare.

71

estate, the turbo 240 was unavailable in the UK and other RHD nations, because it could not be converted to RHD due to the position of the exhaust manifold. It was not cost-effective to re-engineer it. RHD countries would have to wait for something different to arrive in town, which was, by then, well on its way.

There were subtle modifications to the interior, and externally, the impact bumpers became smaller, and a front spoiler was added – a modification which was both aesthetically pleasing, and improved handling and fuel economy. The grille and bonnet of the 240 series cars were also revised to match the more prominent 260 nose. The tall rear lights were updated with a square unit which wrapped around the edges of the car slightly, making the need for a side marker light on the rear panel unnecessary.

In 1983, the range was trimmed, and the 245 was renamed 240, which now applied to both saloon

The GLT (Grand Lux Touring) came along in 1980, and was distinguished by its black mouldings instead of chrome.

The B23E engine was used in the GLT, though some early models had the V6.

For the first time, Volvo introduced a turbocharged, 155hp B21ET engine: the term 'Turbo Brick' was born.

and estate variants. The only V6 left in the range was the estate. The headlamps became standardised across the model range. Previously, the DL, GL, and GLE, and so on, had three different types of headlamps: circular, square and rectangular. Now, the entire 240 series would feature the rectangular style, although slightly modified from the previous design. All of these features simplified the 240 manufacturing process – a much-needed improvement.

The 1983 Volvo offered an adjustable air suspension system that could be inflated either by a

continued on page 76

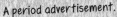

A period advertisement.

From 1983, the standardised designation across saloon/estate variants was '240,' and the cars all featured the 260's raised front.

240 Turbo.

Period advertisement.

The Turbo was never introduced to the UK market due to engineering costs, but the GLT was a strong seller.

The US government bought a batch of 240s, and used them as the safety standard that all other car manufactures would have to reach.

Volvo was not shy about demonstrating the 240 Turbo's get-up-and-go.

garage compressor or the car's very own on-board one: a very useful aid when it came to towing.

Fuel consumption was improving on the 240. Manufacturers claimed figures of up to 39.2mpg on the highway for a manual overdrive GL car, although the three-speed automatic option was considerably lower, at 30.7mpg. In late 1983, a new five-speed gearbox was added to the B23A engine, offering further increases in fuel economy.

The best production year for the 240 was 1984: 85,729 estate variants were sold. Not long after this, in early 1985, the V6-powered 265 was phased out. Management had its eyes firmly on a new model, the 740, and viewed the 240 as something of a throwback to the previous decade. Despite strong sales and global admiration, 1984 was planned to be the final year of

240 production. Thankfully, Volvo wisely refrained from pushing that button. It's a measure of the 240's success that it lasted another nine years past its sell-by date!

In 1985, the Volvo 240 gained further prominence when Italian Gianfranco Brancatelli and Swedish Thomas Lindström raced to victory in the 242 Turbo in the European Touring Car Championship. Today, the 240 has a dedicated following in rally driving.

The next big 240 change occurred in 1986, when, once again, the range welcomed a face-lift. Black plastic trim was added to the lower sections of the car in an attempt to modernise its look. The front end was altered – a flush-fitting

In 1985 the V6-powered 260 was withdrawn, leaving the 240 range, which now had an improved, low friction engine that offered greater fuel economy and durability.

Period advertisement.

Engine range.

Period advertisement.

grille and new bonnet helped smooth the car's boxy appearance, while the tailgates were curved slightly. Many cars were beginning to incorporate microchip technology, and the 240 was no exception.

In April 1988, a separate division was established at Volvo to look after the 240, with a staff of 50. Its task was to carry on the work of updating and improving the model for the remainder of its life, now expected to be a further five years.

A problem with 240s had been that the tailgates tended to rust out. Water collected under the window rubber, causing the edges to rust. In 1989, Volvo designed a new tailgate with a flush bonded rear window, eliminating the problem, as there would be nowhere for the water to sit.

Black seems well-suited to the GLT, but it was not the most popular colour.

A new grille, bonnet, front spoiler, wheel trims, and high-level brake lights were all features of the 1986 face-lift for the 12-year-old car.

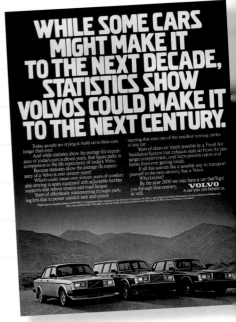

Period advertisement.

Santa Pod raceway in 1994: not much Volvo is left!
Modified old Volvos are becoming increasingly popular,
including V8 conversions.

240 production was planned to end in 1983 to make way for the 700 series, but strong sales proved otherwise.

By 1990, the 240 estate was the most dated car in the Volvo range, but that didn't matter since it sold over 27,000 of them in that year alone. The sporty little Dutch-built 480, with its pop-up headlamps (if they worked) seemed a world away from the hardworking 240. However, slow and steady wins the race: the fact that there are more 240s around than any other estate car of the period proves this case.

In 1991, the 240 received its last revision: it was now the best it had ever been. This would be the model's very last run. Saloon production had stopped; it was just the estate that would carry on for a further two years. A limited edition was brought out, called the 'Torslanda' in UK, whilst on the Continent it was the 'Polar.' All cars were fitted with the economical 2.0-litre engine, most of which were five-speed manual transmissions. The Torslanda was never intended to be a luxury vehicle – quite the opposite, in fact. In my opinion, it was one of the best 240 models ever made. It was all about hard wearing: very basic, and the choice of a very tough material for the seats seemed to make it even more comfortable. With contemporary Volvo green illuminated dials, it felt as modern as possible. In Japan, the last 240s even had airbags fitted. The cars were only available in red, white, or silver, with roof bars fitted as standard. The car is still in demand today, being something of a collector's item. The 240 was also relatively economical: I regularly achieved over 40mpg in mine.

An unusual problem …

The 240 Series became so popular that it created a novel kind of problem for Volvo: demand for both new and secondhand ones was so high that used car dealers had difficulty finding any models to stock their showrooms – in 1983, Volvo resorted to putting out an appeal for well-kept secondhand 240s. By the early 1990s, the 240 estate had become a true cult car – especially in Italy, where it was known as the Polar.

Production finally ended on 5 May 1993: the 240 had outlasted its replacement by one year.

The 240 has been called "the most reliable car in the world" many times. Record-breaking high mileage is just part of the Volvo 240 story.

The dashboard of a Japan-spec 240 Torslanda, circa 1993.

So what made the 240 Volvo estate such a successful and enduring car? A fortuitous combination of reliability, safety and comfort – synonymous with the Volvo brand and a tribute to its outstanding engineering.

The very last Volvo 240 was driven off the production line on 5 May 1993 in front of the press. This was to be the famous old Volvo's bowing-out parade, and it certainly did so in style. Through 19 years of production, and outlasting the 740 model which was brought in to replace it, over 2.8 million cars were sold in over 32 countries. It was rated the safest car in its class many times over.

240 Production 1974-1993: 2,862,573.

7

740|760|960

The 700 series arrived with much to live up to. The 760 saloon was launched in February 1982, and received mixed reviews. It was a radically different car from its predecessors: whereas previous models had built a reputation for solidity and safety, this was intended to promote Volvos as top-of-the-range prestige cars, and not all reviewers thought that was a good move. However, it quickly gained a reputation for good handling (the suspension was designed by Volvo), and, above all, speed. It was powered by a VW 122bhp turbocharged and intercooled six-cylinder diesel engine – very quiet by contemporary diesel standards – which made the 760 one of the world's fastest diesel-powered cars, and a popular choice with European police forces. A new automatic transmission (the AW71 four-speed unit) was introduced, improving fuel consumption by up to 20% on long journeys.

The 760 seemed plush and quite the car to yearn for. Although it wasn't obviously larger than the 240 estate, it certainly felt so inside, where it made every use of a boxy shape to gain further interior space. Its origins can be traced back to 1980, when a new concept was showcased: the VCC (Volvo Concept Car), which looked like a sawn-off 740. This was

In February 1980 Volvo showcased a new estate car concept: the VCC.

Wind tunnel testing: the angular lines and small loading area had both been improved by the time production started.

81

The Volvo estate car – design icon and faithful companion

too extreme for commercial production, but concept cars are all about demonstrating what you have up your sleeve, a sneak peek at future offerings that ensures the public remains excited by and engaged in your brand.

The VCC offered a taste of things to come. For the first time, Volvo had designed a new car as an estate car from the outset.

The interior featured an LCD dashboard, like the Aston Martin Lagonda – but in both cases it was unreliable.

Volvo's reputation for safety is reinforced by constant research and development.

The 740 saloon arrived two years later, in 1984. It would be three years after the original launch before the first estate car was offered: the new 740 and 760 estate series were introduced in 1985. Mechanically, the 740 was quite similar to the 240. However, many things about the 700 series were radically different. Traditional Volvo style had vanished and few curves were in evident in the new design. Whereas before you could trace elements of Volvo car design from the PV series through to the 240, with the angular 740 it was harder to pinpoint Volvo DNA.

The first 700 series estate cars were offered to the US market – no surprise then that the press pictures were taken in typically American landscapes. The 1980s witnessed vast growth in sales of Volvo estate cars, and the 700 range would showcase much innovation. The 740 sits much lower than the 240, and, as such, is a completely different car to drive, with far less body roll and a stiffer suspension. Powered by Volvo's TD24 turbo diesel engine, the 760 GLE became the world's fastest estate car.

The first production car was a 760 GLE. The message was clear: this was an executive estate car.

A strong presence in the North American market meant Volvo was keen to launch its new car there, and, in February 1982, the 760 GLE led the way.

Clive Bengtsson

Many people may recall 'Clive,' Volvo's famous crash test dummy. Far from regarding it as just an item of complex test equipment, Volvo gave it a name, Clive Bengtsson, and a persona, and refers to 'him' as an employee of the corporation. He has been at the forefront in delivering vital impact information and its effect on the human body since 1964. With this data, Volvo constantly improves and pushes the boundaries of safety for its new cars. Today, Clive still exists in various forms and, whilst the software has became vastly more sophisticated over the years, the crash test dummy will always be a part of Volvo.
Clive helped boost Volvo's safety image to a still higher level, when a series of television advertisements in the 1980s featured the crash test dummy driving a Volvo 340 off a building, and landing nose-first to demonstrate the strength of the car. Similar ideas were demonstrated with the 740.

Volvo demonstrates the strength of a 740 Saloon by launching one off a building.

Clive Bengtsson: helping save lives since 1964. During the 1990s, various advertising campaigns made the Volvo crash test dummy a household name.

The 760GLE interior may seem a little dated now, but it's incredibly well built.

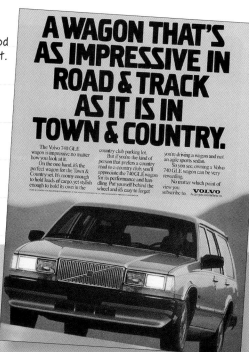

A period advertisement.

The 760 estate was launched at the Chicago Auto Show in February 1985. It was intended purely for the North American market and Volvo had no plans to sell the model elsewhere, but, thankfully, found good reason to do so. Today, traction control often comes as standard, but back then Volvo was the first to offer it, on the 760 – a car that also had ABS. In 1988, the 700 series was gifted with being fully galvanized, and with a whole host of other improvements. Most notably, the revised styling: a new front end with less aggressive edges.

In 1989, a new low-friction engine appeared as a turbo unit with 182bhp. Volvo made every use of its clever and slightly comical marketing, even placing its

True to its origins: a four-cylinder model, the 740, was introduced in 1984. Priced between a 240 and 760, the car was a desirable option.

car next to a Lamborghini Countach. Turbo power was now a key component of Volvo cars, and would take the brand to new heights. Throughout the decade, the 700 series would feature more and more electronic aids, from climate control to electronic ignition, in line with other luxury models. The 740 played an important role for Volvo, providing much consumer information for the company's next project. As with the 240, the 760 was also produced in other factories. In Canada the Halifax plant supplied the North American market, making Volvo the biggest importer to that market at the time. The Belgium plant at Ghant, where the 300 series cars were manufactured, took on the premium model, and, in Sweden, production ran from the Kalmar plant.

There was little external difference between a high-spec 740 and a 760.

The 740GLT featured a new twin-cam 16-valve engine with 155hp: a wolf in sheep's clothing.

Between 1985 and 1990, just over 37,000 top-of-the-range 760 GLE models were produced. The V6-powered 760 remained in production until 1990, when it was finally withdrawn from the range. Meanwhile, in 1992 the 700 series received a face-lift – and even a new name: the 940. With a subtle new redesign, it brought the '80s car into the '90s, with a soft dash and updated dials, trim, wheels and interior aspects. The Volvo 940 was essentially a harmonious mix of old and new. Some of its components could be traced back to the 240, while its underpinning was of the 740.

Although production of the 740 officially ended in 1992, its last incarnation would survive for a further six years: the 960 was visually identical to the 740 when it was introduced in 1990 and shared many of its attributes, but was powered by an all-new in-line six-cylinder engine. It introduced a number of new safety features, including its new Side Impact Protection System (SIPS), a three-point inertia-reel seat belt, an adjustable third head restraint in the middle of the rear seat, and an optional integrated child seat in the rear arm rest.

It was a popular car on both sides of the Atlantic, and as far afield as Australia and Asia. In the early 90s, it was selling well in all markets. The model did require updating, though, and a brilliantly simple method was used to do this in 1985, when it was substantially revised, making the car look so much more appealing in the process.

Both the saloon and estate now had full body-coloured bumpers: the drab grey plastic trim had been cast aside. A new front end with narrow headlamps and a lower nose transformed the car's boxy appearance. It looked like a contemporary American sedan, and that's exactly what Volvo wanted.

Inside, the new 960 was also pleasantly revised. As a 1991 Volvo press release put it: "Both orthopedically designed front bucket seats are power operated with three memory positions. All seating surfaces are leather. An automatic climate control system regulates cabin temperature, while a six-speaker AM/FM stereo cassette system fills the air with sound. Power-operated features include sunroof, windows, remote mirrors and antenna ... Think of it as inconspicuous consumption ... a very satisfying concept in these times."

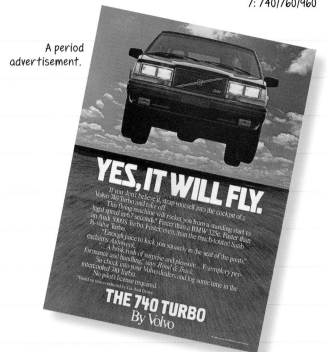

A period advertisement.

The 2.3-litre B23ET turbo engine of the 740 had 173bhp. Later, low friction engines would increase that to 182bhp.

The chassis development in the new 960 improved the car's handling, benefiting from the technological advances made with the new 850 (see Chapter 8).

The 960 performed as well as it looked, and what a car it was! The 3.0-litre straight-six engine delivered effortless power, whilst being utterly comfortable to drive. A smaller 2.5-litre engine was also offered, but most preferred the larger power unit.

You could be forgiven for thinking that the 960 series was just a stop gap before the 850 estate entered the showrooms: the reality is that it was anything but. The 960 became the flagship of the brand: it was chosen by royal families, both in the UK and Sweden, right up until its last breath. People felt a lot of affection for this car. In some ways, it felt more like a traditional Volvo than a modern offering. The 960 was one of those cars with a soul and a sense of having being hand-crafted. For many loyal Volvo drivers, the 960 made us feel nostalgic, particularly when we chose to spend a large percentage of our lives in our vehicles for one reason or another.

With the introduction of the new range of V cars (the V40, and the 850's replacement – the V70), it was necessary that the 960 underwent one final change. In 1997, the 960 became the V90, with only minor changes: clear indicator lenses to rear light clusters, and a few more colour options. It is a very rare vehicle today, and one that should be preserved.

Many 960s have entered a new life as modified custom cars for the growing Volvo scene, which attracts a similar crowd to VW, but on a smaller scale. Customising old Volvos is a very underrated part of car culture, and it is fast becoming the customisers' choice over German machines.

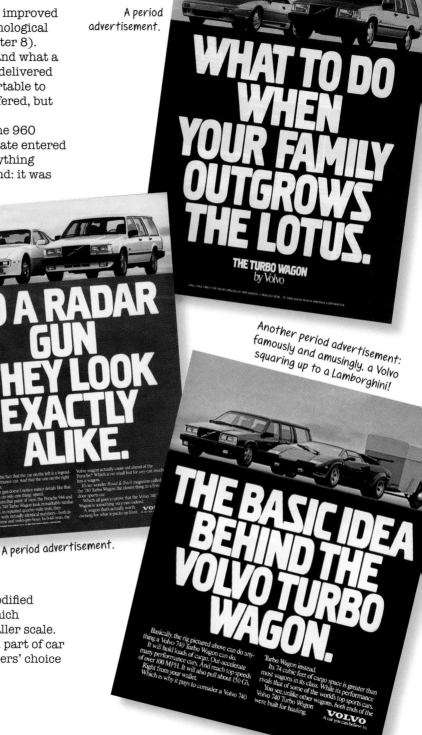

A period advertisement.

A period advertisement.

Another period advertisement: famously and amusingly, a Volvo squaring up to a Lamborghini!

760 production ended in 1990.

The 1989 face-lift brought a new grille and bonnet.

Volvo took the matter of corrosion very seriously;
rustproofing and paint finish was meticulously applied.

What better advertisement for the job!

The 10,000,000 Volvo car to roll off the production line was a 960; but now a new era had arrived for Volvo. Its image was changing, and the Volvo estate story took a new direction.

740/760 Production 1982-1990: 396,397.
960 Estate Production 1990-1996: 83,238.
V90 Production 1996-1998: 9067.

The 1985 780 Coupé: only really intended for the US market and selective European ones. 8518 were produced between 1985–1990.

The 1995 960 had it all – German competitors kept Volvo on its toes. Its pedigree can be traced back to 1980, but the 960 was more than just another face-lift.

In 1990, the 700 series became the 940 and 960. Whilst the cars were fundamentally the same, they gained various enhancements.

One last revision came in 1996: the 960 became the V90, and production lasted for two years. It was to be the very last rear-wheel drive Volvo.

8 850 – the car of change

In June 1991, the much-awaited 850 GLT hit the European market.

Radically different front anything Volvo had produced before, it was clear that the marque was looking to step into a new territory once again. The 850 was the first front-wheel drive vehicle from Volvo to be sold in North America, and also the first all-wheel drive Volvo. The 850 was given a rapturous reception; seldom has a new car won so many awards. Upon its launch, the 850 was tagged: 'A dynamic car with four world-beating breakthroughs' – those being the newly developed five cylinder transverse engine, SIPS (Side Impact Protection System), ARH (self-adjusting seat belt tensioners), and the sophisticated Delta-link rear axle, combining the ride comfort and responsiveness of independent suspension with the security of a live rear axle.

The 850's origins stretched right back to 1978, when Volvo began a long-term project to design a radically new, economical car using all its latest technology. The car would also be front-wheel drive, something that was becoming more popular at the time. As well as new car development, the project would use new production methods, new materials and new plants.

Period advertisement: Volvo becomes aspirational.

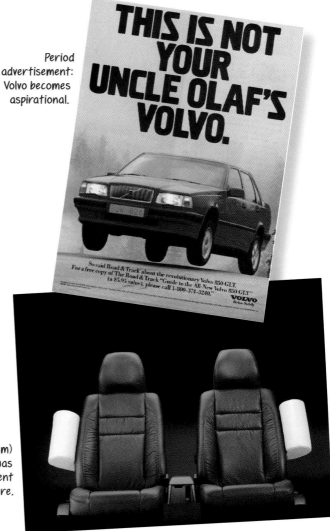

SIPS (Side Impact Protection System) included side airbags in 1995. Volvo was the first manufacturer to implement this safety feature.

Designated Project Galaxy, two cars were planned for development simultaneously: a smaller car of around 1000kg curb weight, and a larger car of around 1200kg. The smaller car became the 440 saloon, introduced in 1987 and closely linked to the 480 launched the previous year, which had been the first Volvo car to have front-wheel drive. The larger car was to become the 850.

The Galaxy Project was to be Volvo's most expensive development program, but it would pay off handsomely as that car represented the future of the company.

A particular misconception about the Volvo 850 engine is that Porsche developed it, but this was not the case. Porsche was approached to develop a six-cylinder engine for the 960, and this straight-six 24-valve double-overhead cam engine was introduced in 1991. Porsche was to have an involvement with the 850, but not for a few years yet ...

Many people think that the 850 was Volvo's first front-wheel drive car, when it was in fact the 480 sport. However, the 850 was the first truly global front-wheel drive car from the marque and it didn't stop there: the 850 would be a first for many reasons.

It was not until February 1993 that the 850 estate would go on sale, and, within two years of its launch, the car had received its first face-lift, which included a softer-looking front, smaller grille, larger wheels, improved switchgear and more attractive headlights. The 850 was a truly modern car, with every technological innovation, including twin airbags, ABS, traction control, dual climate control and, a year later in 1995, it was the first car in the world to feature side airbags. Today, these items are standard features on all but the most inexpensive cars but, in the '90s, they were expensive add-ons.

Something else was also simmering away quietly behind closed doors in the early '90s: not in Sweden, but in a small rural hamlet in Oxfordshire, England. TWR (Tom Walkinshaw Racing), a name associated with various heroic race machines of the 1980s such as the Jaguar XJR Silk Cut cars, was recruited by Volvo to work on its new Back on Track project.

Volvo's link to motorsport was not new – during the '80s, 240 turbo saloons were competing hard and well, even against such powerful rivals as Rover's SD1 which had been developed for racing by TWR; and the previous year, in 1993, Swedish engineering firm Steffansson Automotive modified an 850 estate to evaluate whether such a car would be suitable for racing. The answer was clear: not only did the estate platform offer a great deal of versatility, but it looked so controversial that one wondered

Front-wheel drive, all-wheel drive, five cylinders – and more safety systems than anything else on offer – the 850 was at the beginning of a revolution.

if it could ever be taken seriously. The ultimate Q-car, it had an air of mayhem about it, whilst packing a punch around the track to the open-mouthed astonishment of onlookers.

With the blueprints in hand, TWR knew that it had something that was going to shake up touring car racing. The decision to use the estate over the saloon was something of a closely guarded secret, even to the drivers Rickard Rydell and Jan Lammers (who were to become household names on the back of the project).

You may think that an estate car is not suitable for motorsport, being heavier than a saloon, but due to the large surface area of the roof, it has an increased amount of downforce; also the 850 estate was more powerful than the saloon. Volvo chose the estate for its attention-grabbing nature, too. It's also not a surprise to see most pictures of the estate on two wheels.

On 4 April 1994, 'Back on Track' went into action: two liveried Volvo 850 estate cars joined the line-up at Thruxton in Southern England. It was the start of the season of the most prestigious standard car series, the British Touring Car Championship (BTCC). The idea of using estate cars was a huge success from the outset. They attracted a great deal of attention, and

The 850 estate was launched in 1993, although the 960 was still in production, and the last 240s had just left the showroom.

challenged Volvo's image in a positive way, particularly in the UK. Volvo wanted to demonstrate that it was possible to combine practicality with fun. Apparently, in one heat, the team even placed a large stuffed collie in the boot during the parade lap to wind up the opposition. Volvo injected a much needed sense of lightheartedness in what can be an ego-dominated world of arrogance and snobbery. 1994 was my favourite year for BTCC mainly for this reason.

The TWR 850 deserves recognition for the engineering that went into producing it, too, though this has rarely been properly acknowledged. Sadly, the 850 estate's contribution to motorsport was shortlived: in 1995, the FIA changed the rules on aerodynamic advances, and the estate cars were excluded. From then on TWR entered Volvo saloon variants.

The 20-valve turbo engine used in the T5 – a car wtih an incredible 150mph top speed, it quickly gained the admiration of European police forces.

94

I wonder if pressure had been placed on the FIA from other competitors to get the Volvo estates off the track?

After the 850 series, the S40 carried the competitive beacon for Volvo, but it's the 850 estate that everyone really remembers today. A legend was born, and eventually handed back to Gothenburg, where one of these original race 850 estate cars can be seen at the Volvo museum. If you do get the chance to have a look, you will be amazed at just how low it sits.

The GLT would have been fun in the snow with its 190bhp.

Volvo wasn't new to racing, it just wasn't in the mainstream. Then along came the British Touring Car Championship, and Volvo entered two 850 estates.

With a larger surface area than the saloon, the estate created more downforce.

In most pictures of the racing 850s, they're cornering on two wheels!

There are plenty of cases of products being rebranded or having an image change. Celebrities do it all the time. Cars are no exception. As time rolls on, they stagnate or change. Even if the brand still has some good products, sometimes a certain image can stick, and it's very hard to shake that off unless something particularly radical is undertaken.

Radical was a word that must have been written in blood on the walls of the special vehicle department at Volvo in the early 1990s, because in 1995 the marque was catapulted from conventional to tarmac-tearing rule-breaker – enter the T5. It wasn't that it was a completely different car, just that it would appeal to a completely different driver. The 850 T5 was all about performance. This was Volvo's answer to how to poach BMW's M5 clientele. For the first time, a Volvo was electronically limited to a governed speed of 152mph! The interior also gained its race breed inspiration from Porsche, with Alcantara trim in places. The 850 T5-R blended executive refinement with high-performance, and still held to true to what a Volvo estate has always been. Just that now the

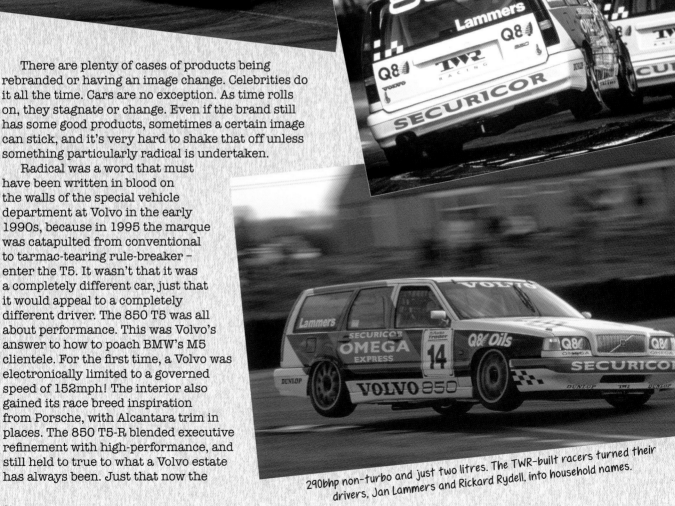

290bhp non-turbo and just two litres. The TWR-built racers turned their drivers, Jan Lammers and Rickard Rydell, into household names.

This car is now on display at the Volvo Museum in Gothenburg. Note how low it sits.

The two Volvo 850 estates at the 1994 British Touring Car Championship.

Sales of the limited edition T5-R were so strong that Volvo built more than twice the number planned: a new breed of Volvo drivers had been created.

happy driver could travel with Volvo levels of safety at speeds up to 150mph. Many European police forces quickly realised the potential a T5 could add to their patrol fleets – forces in the UK were happy to place big orders too.

Today, the Volvo estate provides the backbone for many motorway patrols; it was the T5 that kick-started it all. Having an estate car with the ability to keep up with even the fastest hot hatch gave the police a cheaper (and versatile) option. Who would have imagined a Volvo estate could do that?

Clearly the 850 T5-R represented a major shift for Volvo, a new image was here. Gone was the boxy shape and caravan image. This was the year of spoilers, lowered suspension, and large alloys. The Pirelli P-Zero tyre said it all. Volvo had put a lot of thought into developing a car like the T5-R, and it was perfectly timed: simply put, it was both what people wanted – and also what they thought they wouldn't!

If the T5-R wasn't fast enough, Volvo went one step further, in 1996, when it launched the 850 R. Thanks to the T5-R, Volvo had done very well in rapidly changing its identity. It wanted to create a new car that would be all that the T5-R was, but even better. Better being, by default, faster!

This new incarnation of the 850 platform had real sex appeal. As an advertisement for the R put it, "If power is the ultimate aphrodisiac then prepare to be seduced." For the first time, a Volvo estate was a pin-up. I had a poster of it, myself, on my bedroom wall when I was a teenager. The 850 R was launched in red – bold and seductive, with other colours as options. The R was not just fast, it was an animal! Top speed was claimed as 158mph, although some fans attest to faster speeds.

Inside, the R was a fusion of racing car and luxury, with walnut trim, an alcantara and leather steering wheel, and aluminium pedals. R-branded floor mats and stainless kick plates on the sills reminded you that you were in something special every time you opened the door. A premium 200W eight-speaker sound system was also an option. The R had distinctive new volan 17in wheels.

A fast-appreciating collector's item today, it is the most important modern Volvo of the new generation, simply because it was the car that introduced a new era.

The R was discontinued in 1997, when the new V70 series was brought in to replace the 850. However, there was another 850 model, introduced in 1996, which pushed Volvo into an emerging all-wheel drive (AWD) market. Volvo was built in the land of hard driving, so it was fitting that it would adopt all-wheel drive for its cars. After all, Volvo had been manufacturing military vehicles for many years. However, there was nothing workaday about the 850 AWD setup.

In July 1996, the first AWDs entered the UK market, with limited distribution around the world. It was a glimpse of what was to come. The most obvious target was the Subaru Legacy and Audi A6 Quattro market. However, Volvo had high hopes that it would do more than just appeal to existing Volvo fans but would also appeal drivers of traditional 4x4s. Volvo was creating a new market. Why buy a bulky, gas guzzling, conventional 4x4, when you could have the same capability in a smaller, economical, and more functional package? That was the basic premise of the AWD 850.

The AWD car had increased ground clearance, and front and rear mud flaps added. The 2.5-litre 20-valve

In 1996, the 'R' was born: based on the T5-R, it was much more exclusive, featuring new Volan 17inch wheels, 250bhp and limited to 155mph!

Interior of the fastest production Volvo yet – with light birch dashboard panelling, and alcantara trim on the seats.

light-pressure turbo engine gave the car plenty of torque, aiding towing and light off-road use. At the launch, Volvo claimed 0-62mph in 8.5 seconds with a top speed of 137mph. An innovative system was created to give the car its AWD traction: in normal mode, it gave 95 per cent traction to the front and five per cent to the rear, but, if grip was lost in one wheel, power would shift to those that had the best traction.

850 Estate Production. 1993-1997: 326,068.

All-wheel drive from 1996 made the fast estate car even more capable.

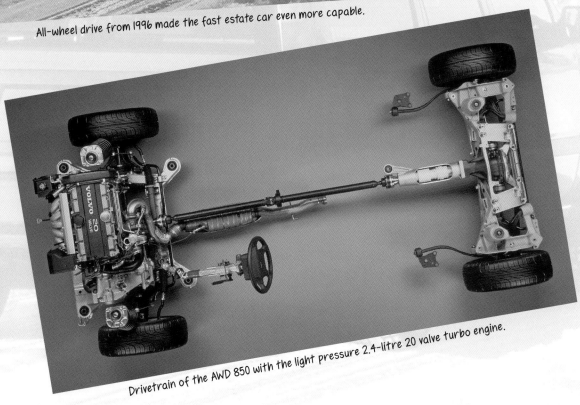

Drivetrain of the AWD 850 with the light pressure 2.4-litre 20 valve turbo engine.

9

V40

The V40 was part of a joint venture between Volvo and Mitsubishi, and manufactured at the Nedcar plant in the Netherlands. It was the first compact estate car from Volvo.

In the summer of 1995, as the Spice Girls signed to Virgin Records, a new small luxury Volvo series was launched. This was a joint venture with Mitsubishi – the Volvo V40 and Mitsubishi Carisma shared a platform and were both manufactured at the Ghant plant in the Netherlands. The V40 was originally intended to be called the S4, but Audi objected as it already used that designation for its A4 sport. Threatened with legal action, Volvo changed the name to S40, with V40 for the saloon and estate.

The compact estate car changed Volvo's image again, appealing to a younger, fashion-conscious market, and showing that Volvo could build a medium-size executive car.

Engines ranged from 1587cc to 1948cc-litre petrol, with a 1870cc turbo diesel later on. The 1.9-litre turbo diesel was the Renault power plant carried over from the old 440 model. The small Volvo estate was an inventive package but, as good as it was, it took five years to break into the North American market. In 2000, the V40 received a face-lift to increase its appeal. Chrome door handles, bumper trim, and a black grille transformed its appearance. Later cars also
continued on page 105

The Volvo 480 sports hatch was manufactured in the same plant – this concept convertible that made it to production.

The Volvo estate car – design icon and faithful companion

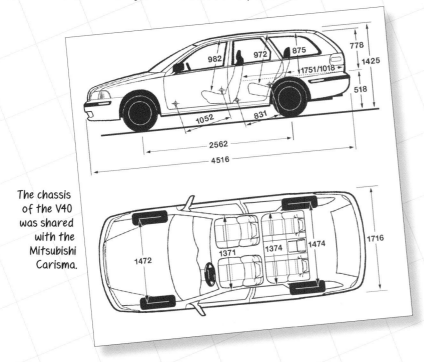

The chassis of the V40 was shared with the Mitsubishi Carisma.

Although smaller than its 850 brother, the V40 was still a true estate car. It meant that Volvo could now compete with cars such as the BMW 3 series.

The V40 was popular with younger drivers with an active lifestyle.

The Volvo estate car – design icon and faithful companion

Side impact crash testing a V40 against a heavy S80 saloon.

In 2001 a new phase two V40 went on sale with various revisions, including inflatable curtain and two-stage airbags.

V40 Production ended in 2004 and by that time it was a smart looking car.

Interior of a 2004 model V40. The V40's interior never matched the quality of a V70.

Phase two car with clear indicator lenses.

featured WHIPS (Whiplash Protection System), and further interior enhancements, including additional controls, and updated fascia panels. Handling was improved by widening the front track by 18mm, which enabled larger tyres to be fitted.

In 1999, Volvo offered a hot V40, with the 2.0-litre turbo engine giving 200bhp and a claimed top speed of 146mph, plus a 0-60 time of 7.1 seconds – nearly double its entry edition's power.

In 2001, Volvo launched a new range of dual-fuelled vehicles, which could run on gas as well as petrol. Prominent among these was the V40. Known as 'bi-fuel' cars, they could run on LPG (Liquid Petroleum Gas, a mixture of propane and butane), which was cheaper to buy than petrol or diesel (though produced lower mpg), and significantly more environmentally-friendly. LPG was all the rage in the early 2000s, and appeared to have a rosy future. However, in the UK, government subsidies ended in 2005, and with uncertainty about long-term government support, vehicle manufacturers gradually phased it out.

Bi-fuel systems also had performance issues. Engines ran hotter, and some aftermarket systems were unreliable. Gas availability was patchy, too, and

looked unlikely to increase, as interest in LPG systems among manufacturers declined.

By 2004, V40 production was being wound down to make room for its replacement, the V50 (see Chapter 13).

V40 Production 1995-2004: 423,491.

10 V70 Classic

The new V70 launched in 1996 was basically a reworked 850, although sleeker and more elegant – styled by British designer Peter Horbury. The V70 was the first step in Volvo's new stylish range, where it would share showroom space with a radical new car for Volvo, the sporty C70 coupé and convertible. The V70 was not just a flashy new estate car but, rather, complemented the growing image of a new, younger Volvo driver looking for performance. The V90 (formerly the 960), which remained in production until 1998, was now appearing dated.

With the popular 850 R gone, the V70 R was introduced in May 1997, and became Volvo's standard-bearing, high-performance estate car. As with previous R models, it featured a leather/alcantara interior. It had a unique front bumper, blue gauge faces for the instrument cluster, and special alloy wheels. All US cars were equipped with 16in alloy wheels. Other markets had 17in either as standard, or as an option. A trunk-mounted CD-changer and navigation system were included. The suspension was new, and firmer shocks were standard. All R models were fitted with

the highest performance engines and came with either automatic or manual transmission, and with front-wheel drive or all-wheel drive.

In 1999, the V70 received a few updates, mainly to interior and badging. The V70 R was

The 1997 V70 was an even more rewarding drive than the 850. The V nomenclature came into the Volvo range ('V' for versatility).

A timeless design: this image was used on various marketing material.

Transporting a cello without a case is not recommended, but the fold-flat front passenger seat was an inspired addition.

The comfortable and well-finished V70 interior: very hard wearing and solid – many owners favour the classic for that reason.

Surprisingly agile for such a big car – the motoring press praised the V70's driving position.

The AWD 850 established a new kind of estate car, naturally the V70 continued the legacy.

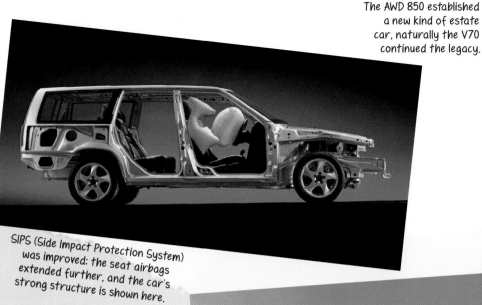

SIPS (Side Impact Protection System) was improved: the seat airbags extended further, and the car's strong structure is shown here.

presented with a striking new colour option – Laser Blue – which really made it stand out. The strangely popular Saffron was left out in 1999, although it had been a colour option previously.

In 2000, a new 2.4L engine was introduced, and power was upgraded to 265bhp. Annoyingly, Volvo only offered it with four-speed automatic transmission, although I believe there were some special-order manual examples.

The V70 classic (as it is referred to now) was a very good car indeed. Its build quality was typically rugged and dependable, with good quality furnishings. I once owned a very early example, one of the first in the UK. Despite carrying everything from old

The beautiful C70 convertible shared much of the V70 platform.

kitchen units to a 1930 Austin 7 in bits, it soaked up the miles and clocked 280,000 miles before bowing out. Many people view this car as one of the best Volvos ever made.

In 1997, Volvo launched the V70 XC ('cross country') – a new breed of car that combined the luxury and dynamics of an estate car with the versatility of AWD. It had extra ground clearance to handle rough terrain. Raised suspension, roof rails, lots of ugly black plastic trim, and smaller alloy wheels signalled that the XC was all about adventure. It featured AWD as standard. It also had an interior grab handle for the front passenger.

With the XC, Volvo had developed a real alternative to a traditional SUV (Sports Utility Vehicle), something that was going to feature in its model line up from that point forward.

The V70 classic was one of the most adaptable vehicles on the market. If we compare the R and the XC side-by-side, they are essentially the same car, but in two completely different styles.

XC V70 offered an alternative to a traditional 4x4. Designed to cope with deep snow, it had a raised chassis and hard-wearing black mouldings.

The Volvo estate car was becoming even more versatile.

A new V70 R was launched – this time with AWD and 265bhp.

Production of the V70 classic ended in 2000, as a new estate car was waiting at Gothenburg. If we include the 850 as part of the V70 story, then we could say that it had a seven-year run, or just four years as the reworked V70 – quite short, given what it had brought to the market. The V range was now an established series for Volvo.

V70 Classic Production 1996-2000: 373,689.

The Saffron launch colour of the V70 R: production of the R ended in 2000.

Laser Blue made the R look special, although it was a rare colour choice.

11 V70 P2

A new millennium, a new car: the new V70. It was derived from the S80 executive saloon, launched in 1998, which had been built on a new unibody, called the P2 platform, and claimed by Volvo to be as much as 70% more rigid than its predecessor. Outlandishly bold and charismatic, the V70 drew on over half a century of Volvo design. Its heritage was instantly recognisable from its V-shaped bonnet, low grille and boxy rear end. Its prominent shoulder lines echoed the S80, and the rounded curves of its side profile were particularly

attractive. Styled by Peter Horbury, this was the most aerodynamic Volvo estate car yet, and also included more sophisticated electronics, and a further range of options – including an ingenious fold-out picnic table which turned the rear into a pleasant place to watch a sunset over a small glass of wine. With its almost-vertical tailgate, the wonderful new V70 ensured that every little bit of interior space was available, making it popular as an upmarket van. As Peter Horbury described it later: "Imagine the front end of an E-type Jaguar married to the back end of a Ford Transit van. With the Volvo V70, we have tried to combine the two."

[Volvo press release 2006]

The V70 wasn't without its faults: the turning radius was terrible; even the cheapest alternative offerings put it to shame, and many a long-standing Volvo owner became stuck when trying to negotiate a tight turn. That aside, the car was, and still is, very good.

Inside, the V70 was about as modern as the year 2000 would permit. If it was only a tiny bit bigger on paper than its predecessor, but it certainly felt a whole lot more. Volvo has and continues to be a leader in thinking about driver and family needs. Great design touches included split folding rear seats, and a grocery bag holder to keep shopping secure and upright during travel. Some also featured a waste bag holder/bottle holder for rear passengers, while options included

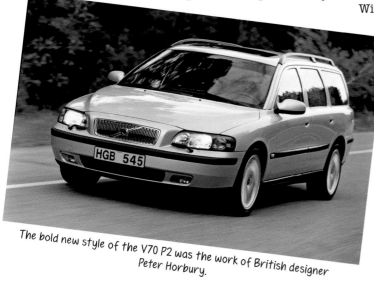

The bold new style of the V70 P2 was the work of British designer Peter Horbury.

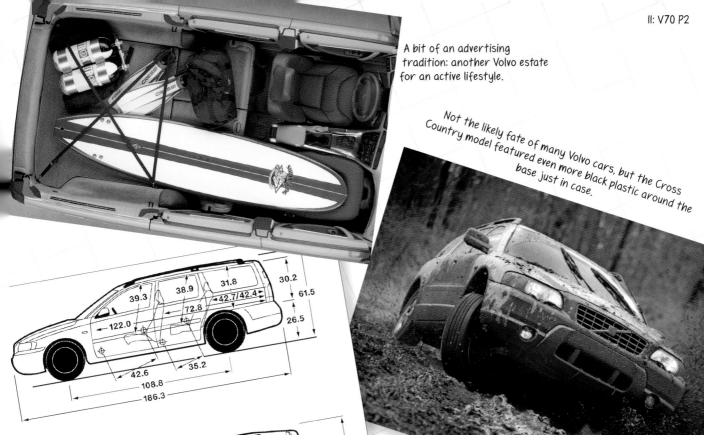

A bit of an advertising tradition: another Volvo estate for an active lifestyle.

Not the likely fate of many Volvo cars, but the Cross Country model featured even more black plastic around the base just in case.

The new V70 was a larger car than the classic, and used new bonded construction in some areas, which increased strength and reduced weight.

Cutaway of the V70 P2, showing airbag deployment and the car·s strong structure.

The perfect location for an off-road Volvo.

integrated booster seats for both outer rear seats, and a pop-up folding table or child seat within the centre rear armrest.

If you thought the old V70 XC had too much black plastic, then the new one would rile you even more. It was everywhere on this car: profile wheel arches, door bottoms, sills, and front and rear unpainted bumpers – but it was there for good reason: the lower parts of the

The 2002 ACC2 (Adventure Concept Car) – a stripped-out off-road winter racer packed with all of the latest technological innovations, and powered by a 300bhp engine. Many of its features would find their way into Volvo's new model.

The handy fold-out table of the V70 – perfect for scenic breaks.

The PCC (Performance Concept Car) whetted people's appetite once again for a fast Volvo. The next R was to come.

The Volvo V70 R
October 2002

VOLVO
Press Office 01628 422288
© copyright for editorial purposes only

A UK press release for the new V70 R.

vehicle would bear the brunt of off-road conditions, and would have to be tough and long-lasting. Shiny paintwork is nice, but quite impractical in those situations. However the V70 XC was never intended to be a fully off-road vehicle in the style of a traditional 4x4.

For 2003, the model was renamed to XC70, in keeping with Volvo's newly-introduced XC90 (see Chapter 12). Note: For the third generation XC70, launched in 2008, a new feature was introduced, called 'hill-descent-control' (HDC) which automatically limited speed on steep inclines without the driver having to use the brake. This meant the driver was able to utilise the accelerator pedal on its own to control the car's speed – particularly useful on steep embankments or when launching a boat from a wet slipway, for example.

For the first time in the history of the Volvo estate there was no direct saloon version of the V70. (The S80 shared many of its systems, but was a high-end luxury saloon, not a directly-equivalent family sedan.) A welcome feature was a lever on the passenger front seat, which, when pulled, made the backrest fold flat – ideal for extra long loads, such as surf boards and camp beds!

Passenger safety has always been the element that puts Volvo ahead of its competitors. As standard, the V70 featured three types of airbag: seat-mounted SIPS (Side Impact Protection System), WHIPS (Whiplash Protection System) and IC (Inflatable Curtain), which

With three adaptive chassis settings available at the touch of a button, the R's sophisticated suspension gave it the handling attributes of a true race car.

would erupt from the headlining along the sides of the car).

As good as the new car was, there were cloudy days ahead for Volvo cars. In 1999, Ford purchased Volvo Cars Corporation (not to be confused with anything else Volvo) for the sum of $6.45 billion, beating Fiat and VW to the table. Ford purchased Volvo Cars to add to its stable of high profile brands, such as Aston Martin and Jaguar, under the banner of its Premier Automotive Group.

It was not a success. Ford wanted Volvo not just because it was a profitable marque, but to share everything it did well with the other brands in the group. Although Volvo management maintained some freedom, it had to answer to Detroit, making compromises that damaged the brand's identity.

Some good things did come out of the Ford relationship: Ford wanted to push

Now with 300bhp, the V70 really was safety fast.

Take a good look, because you won't see it again: the P2 R was to be the last high performance V70.

The 2003 VCC concept showcased some very bold and distinctive ideas.

Volvo's sponsorship of the Ocean Race led to a range of special edition cars.

Volvo further upmarket, to compete with the lower specification Mercedes and BMW saloons, estates and SUV crossovers. This resulted in the luxurious second generation Volvo S80, and the small premium crossover Volvo XC60. However, with Ford, it was all about horizontal synergies between the companies. An S80 and a Mondeo were essentially the same car, and this move towards standardisation did not sit well with Volvo management, or go down well with Volvo

buyers. Ford was to sell Volvo Car Corporation in 2010 for a mere $1.8 billion to the Chinese Geely Automobile Holdings, representing a significant loss.

Thankfully, the V70 managed to escape without too much interference, as its development was pretty much complete by the time Ford assumed control.

With petrol engines becoming less popular, in 2001 Volvo had at last developed its own diesel engine to replace the aging Volkswagen unit it had been using

In 2004, the V70 underwent a face-lift, with new clear indicator lenses, and different bumper mouldings and wheels.

A space-inspired gearlever in the manual cars, and updated materials for the interior, from the 2004 face-lift.

since the introduction of the 850. Based on the Volvo Modular Engine, the D5 was a five-cylinder, all-aluminium engine with 20 valves and twin overhead camshafts. The first D5 appeared in the new P2 V70s. However, the XC70 did not benefit from the D5 engine in the North American market.

Interestingly, a new car buyer's survey in 2002 established that the typical V70 customer was university educated, a company director or retired, and aged between 35 and 64. In 2003, the same source claimed that the five best-selling countries for the V70 were Sweden, USA, Germany, UK, and Japan.

Two new R variants were launched in 2002: the S60 R saloon and V70 R estate. Both shared the same colour combinations of orange leather interiors, and light turquoise paint called Flash Green. Power was increased to 300bhp, with AWD and a six-speed manual gearbox, giving a 0-60 time of 5.4 seconds; not bad for something that would be very much at home at a caravan site. Its Four-C (Continuously Controlled Chassis Concept) suspension had three levels of firmness, delivered at the touch of a button: Comfort, Sport, and Advanced Sport.

In its earliest incarnation, the Comfort setting caused the V70 R to pitch and roll alarmingly, and lurch around corners in an unsettling fashion. However, in its later configuration, introduced in 2005, I seem to recall that the car's handling felt amazing in Sport mode – it hugged each corner and felt like a pure driver's car. If you didn't notice the Brembo calipers when you stepped into the car, you certainly would when you slammed on the brakes!

Externally, the car's stance remained quite conservative. It came with smaller door mirrors and rear spoiler, and a lower front spoiler with a matt black grille. As with all of these pure R models, this one was

2005 saw the introduction of a lightly face-lifted V70, with a more executive feel – fancy chrome trim around the bumpers, clear indicator lenses, brushed aluminium inserts, and the Volvo logos.

Since 1998, Volvo had been the sponsor of a prestigious round the world sailing race: the Volvo Ocean Race. Fitting, then, that in 2005 it should choose to produce a limited edition of adventure cars within the V70, XC, and XC90 range, named 'Ocean Race Series.' Tahiti Blue was the colour, with Ocean Race badging, blue trim inserts, and unique wheels. Other than that, the cars were standard.

destined to be a classic of the future (especially in its launch colour). The UK price at the time of launch at the British International Motor Show was £38,000.

The sixth gear on the P2 really made a difference to both consumption and engine noise, not that any of the engines were particularly noisy at cruising speed. The new automatic Geartronic was introduced (reliable when new, but it can be troublesome and costly to repair now, unless it has been well looked after).

The Volvo V70 won an array of awards, including *What Car?* magazine's 'Estate Car of the Year' several years running, but by 2007, that was it for the P2. It had pushed the estate car concept further than ever before, pioneering diesel technology with increased comfort, style, and pace.

V70 P2 Production 1999-2007: 929,794.

12 XC90

The dramatic arrival of the XC90 in January 2002 marked Volvo's move into an entirely new market segment: that of the SUV. Although in some ways a natural progression from the XC variants of previous Volvo estate cars, it was Volvo's first purpose-designed, off-road vehicle. It was also the most flexible car the company had ever built. It seated up to seven passengers, all equally protected by Volvo's advanced safety systems, regardless of where they were in the car. It drove like a car, but loaded like a van, thanks to its generous cabin height, and easily-accessible cargo space with a split-folding tailgate that harked back to the Amazon estate of the early '60s.

Launched at the 2002 American International Auto Show, the XC90 was an immediate success.

Body structure and safety systems of the XC90.

With all the seats folded flat, load space is very impressive.

121

The Volvo estate car – design icon and faithful companion

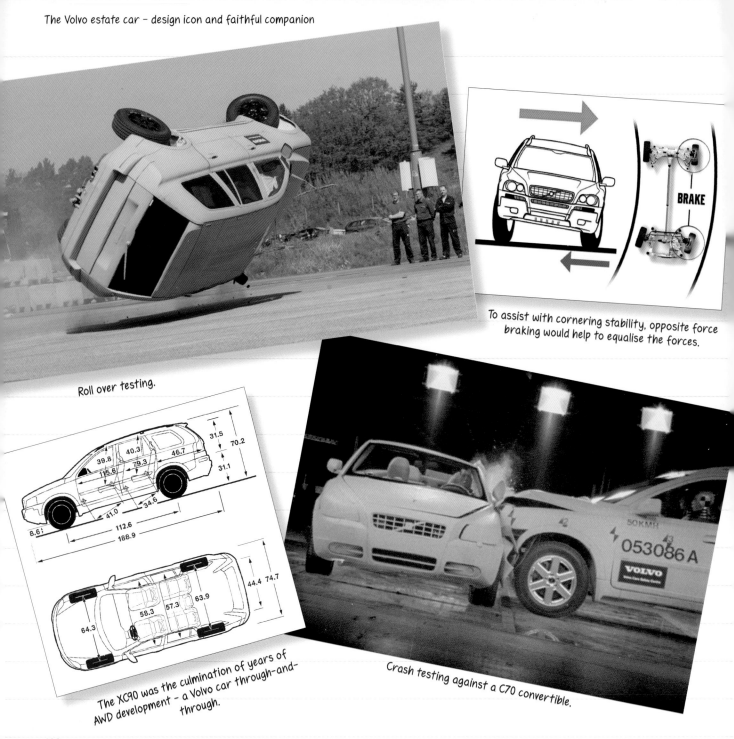

To assist with cornering stability, opposite force braking would help to equalise the forces.

Roll over testing.

The XC90 was the culmination of years of AWD development – a Volvo car through-and-through.

Crash testing against a C70 convertible.

Targeted strongly at the US market, it was unveiled at the 2002 Detroit Auto Show to great acclaim, and was an instant success: indeed, in 2005, it was Volvo's best-selling model in the US and around the world. It was so popular, in fact, that demand far outstripped supply, and secondhand examples sold for a premium.

The XC90 used the P2 platform of the S80 and V70, and the T6 had a surprisingly-low weight for a six-cylinder car (just over 2100kg), thanks to its clever use of light materials and construction. Its styling was instantly recognisable as Volvo. There were two engine options for the US, the 2.5 turbo and twin turbo T6, both petrol. In European markets, the options were the 163bhp D5 and 272bhp T6. Just about every Volvo-conceived safety system was built into the 4x4, and it was voted SUV of the year in America at its launch. Many owners love the XC90 because of its all-round practicality for the family, complete with lots of child-friendly features.

With six adult-sized passenger seats, the XC90 was the first seven-seater Volvo since the 1940s. In order to get the car as low to the ground as possible, whilst still retaining 4x4-type ground clearance, another new feature was introduced: RSC (Roll Stability Control), which used a gyro-sensor to monitor the car's roll speed and angle. If necessary, the system would stabilise any excessive body roll by braking the outside wheels. In 2004, the UK market got the 2.5 turbo petrol (gasoline) engine, which was a compromise between the economy of the D5 and the performance of the T6, with the option of a six-speed manual transmission. At this point, the price for an XC90 ranged from £31,230 for the basic model to £45,665 for the T6 Executive. A top speed of 130mph was as fast as such a car would need to be, although by today's SUV standards it's left in the past.

In the summer of 2005, the D5's power output was increased to 183bhp, as well as for the Volvo Ocean Race series XC90 model. A new V8 engine was added, an idea Volvo had sitting on the shelf for decades. Developed by Yamaha (of all companies), the engine was unique in being a transverse unit. The V8 was designed in Sweden and built in Japan, but it never really realised

US-specification dashboard.

its potential. The V8 XC90 was dropped with the change of ownership from Ford to Geely. Many of the V8 cars that survive today have been adapted by their owners, with uprated exhaust systems and such. One wonders what Volvo Special Vehicles could have done if it had unlimited time and resources at the time. Nonetheless, even the raw V8 could be an interesting engine to play around with today, as the cars become affordable.

There was a minor face-lift in 2006, offering little change visually. As the years progressed, other refinements were made, but the XC90 remained largely unchanged from then onwards, ceasing production in 2014.

It had been a runaway success. With the cool of a Land Rover Discovery, but immensely more practical for domestic use, families the world over raved about it, and with good reason.

XC90 Classic 2002-2014: 703,325.

Harking back to the Amazon estate: a two-piece tailgate.

The last XC90s featuring body-coloured bumpers: the 4x4 segment had expanded, with more cars being acquired for urban use than for off-road driving.

MTU 967

13 V50

Ford had always intended to create a Volvo car that would share its platform with other Ford brands, and in 2003 it did so with the V50. This was part of the Ford C1 platform, which included the Ford Focus, Mazda 3, and even the Land Rover Freelander. Purists criticise it for being a Ford in disguise, while others simply love it. Be that as it may, the V50 brought some innovations to Volvo that would permeate the rest of the Volvo range. It was intended as the replacement for the V40 (which ceased production in 2004). The V40 was still popular, but had become dated, and had been tarted up just about as much as it could be. Whilst the V50 did share Ford parts, it was unmistakably a Volvo estate. Slab-sided and showing distinct Volvo characteristics, it was a strong car, and did not compromise on safety just because it was a cheaper vehicle.

The small V50 offered a sense of V70 style – closer in design and specification to the larger V70 than its predecessor had been – recognisably Scandinavian, with an emphasis on clean lines and stylish functionality. It was marketed as a sporty,

The V50's bold stylish Scandinavian design appealed to people who weren't typical Volvo buyers.

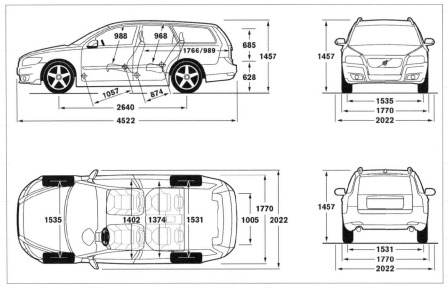

Many of the V50's components were shared with existing Ford products, which was a mixed blessing.

compact car with large-car attributes. The minimalist interior felt spacious and included a free-floating centre console – unique to the range at the time, which also included the S40 saloon and C70 convertible. (The C70 had debuted in 1997, and the 1997 movie *The Saint* featured a C70 – a fitting tribute to the P1800, which was famously Roger Moore's car in the original TV series.) The Volvo V50 was also launched with specially developed upholstery material – T-Tec – inspired by sportswear accessories. Advertising also emphasised its streamlined 'boat' profile, which gave it a compact and athletic appearance. Henrik Otto, Volvo Car's Design Director described the range as "Ready for take-off!" A 20mm lowering kit was part of a sports option.

The following year, Volvo showcased something special – not intended for production, more to promote the newly established Volvo Special Vehicles department in Gothenburg, Sweden. The V50 SV (Special Vehicle) was launched at the 2004 Specialty Equipment Manufacturers Association (SEMA) trade show in Las Vegas.

The SEMA show is one of America's leading catwalks of automotive style, the all-American dream positively embraces all who visit and exhibits. There are very few motor shows like this that actively combine hot rod, pro-street, and mainstream manufacturers all under one roof, with one element being key: individuality.

Based on the production version of the 2005 V50 T5 AWD activity sportswagon, the high-performance V50 SV was targeted at a younger audience that traditionally would have ignored the Volvo brand, seeing it as safe but dull. It was a one-off, designed to see just how far Volvo's Special Vehicles department could push the boundaries. As Volvo Car USA put it, "While Volvo has no plans of offering the V50 SV parts or materials through its retailer network, it gives young enthusiasts and the aftermarket companies that cater to them a thought provoking 'launching pad' to get their creative juices flowing. Understated and refined, the Volvo V50 SV has what it takes to turn heads and handle well on the race track."

This was a bold step for Volvo and one that demonstrates its forward-thinking. The V50 SV packed the S60 R engine with an extra 40hp, totalling 340hp and with a 0-60 time of 5.5 seconds. Not bad for an off-the-shelf modified car, given that the SEMA show has more horsepower than the Grand National. The SV hosted a whole range of alterations, including a larger turbo, racing suspension (lower by 12mm), and AP calipers to the front.

The V50 estate car would have been a completely different concept without Ford's involvement – whether better or worse, is hard to discern. It gained the five-star Euro NCAP rating expected from a Volvo. A VW Golf estate had more room, but lacked the style and individuality of the V50. While, in diesel mode, with the smaller 1.6-litre, up to 74mpg was achievable – a far cry from the less-than-impressive figures of 20 years earlier. A very smooth and easy drive, you could forget that the back end was an estate, especially the sporty R-Design package.

Compact interior
of the V50.

The V50's floating centre
console featured a Bang &
Olufsen sound system.

The V50 shared
its chassis with
the Ford Focus,
which was a good
car; one of the
better Ford models
of the time.

A cheaper car, but no less a Volvo for that!

Technology led the way, and the V50 was a guinea pig for innovation. Many of its features found their way onto the next generation P3 V70. Even part of the CAN (Controller Area Network) wiring harness was used within the Aston Martin DB9 and Vantage.

The Volvo logo had been updated in 2006, and became standard across the range of Volvo vehicles. On the V50 the change was most noticeable, because of its smaller grille.

In 2008, the V50 was updated slightly, featuring further options including the D5 with the six-speed gearbox as per V70, and a more economical 1.8-litre petrol engine. The V50 T5 with 225hp in manual form was a very lively car. Ford utilised much of this innovation in its Focus ST hot hatch, which promoted everything anathema to Volvo in a loud a brash manner. In the US market, the performance V50 was only available in AWD automatic with the new R-Design package, which was now just a sporty trim package with a hint of a high octane.

By 2010, the V50 had reached its technological peak; the following year, engine and transmission options were reduced. The V50 was on its way out – production stopped in 2011.

V50 Production 2003-2011: 509,224.

Volvo V50 SV concept had a modified S60 R engine, giving 340bhp.

14 V70 P3

In 2011, with Volvo still under Ford's umbrella, the V70 did not escape cost-cutting. The previous model had just about managed to avoid it, but things were going to change. As with the V50, the V70 P3 was designed to share parts with other models across the Ford range. Its petrol engines were to be found in Mazdas, and various Ford models.

The new P3 was a bigger car than the P2 model (see Chapter 11), being 120mm longer, 60mm wider, and 80mm taller. The interior featured a free-floating console, as previously seen on the V50. The sweeping curves of the older model had been replaced with an almost clinical sombre feel, straight-edged and somewhat harsh. The cabin had a cheaper feel, but many owners prefer it to that of the older car. In fact, there is quite a debate among Volvo owners as to which is actually the better car, and many owners have mixed feelings, especially when it comes to reliability.

Another new feature on the P3 was the parking brake button – a characteristic of many modern cars – replacing the old-style lever. Many of the V70 P3's innovations came from the little C30 hatchback.

In May 2008, Volvo launched a new package for the V70: 'R-Design,' in place of the high-performance 'R' version of its cars. This was a massive let down for loyal 'R' customers – not to mention the many Volvo enthusiasts who aspired to own such a car. The P3 would not include a high-performance version in its line up. The R-Design was not a package that could be ordered on any V70, but neither was it a range-topping vehicle in itself. Instead, it would be a cosmetic enhancement only. It gave the driver the look of an 'R' Volvo, but that was just a clever use of plastics. Where Audi had S-Line for its sports packages, Volvo now offered R-Design to compete. The R-Design

Slightly larger than the model it replaced, the 2008 V70 featured the floating centre console. Despite its sporty look, it was anything but.

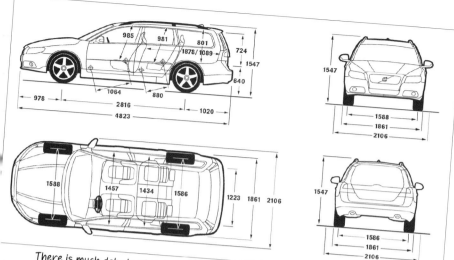

There is much debate about which is the best V70 model: the R-Design package was introduced, replacing the performance 'R' Volvos of the past.

A 2008 UK-specification interior.

package proved a very successful product for Volvo, and extended right across the range. With a variety of sporty-looking options, interior finishes and colours, the V70 remains the descendant of the original high-performance 850 R.

However all was not lost in terms of performance: with the 3.0-litre T6 engine, the car had a top speed of 152mph and a 0–60 time of 6.7 seconds. The T6 engine was made in Wales, and gave the V70 real oomph.

As with previous models, there was a range of engines to choose from for the new V70, including two FlexiFuel versions, powered by E85, a fuel that was 85 percent bioethanol, 15 percent petrol, and could be made from sources such as sugar cane, corn, wheat, sugar-beet and cellulose. (Carbon dioxide emissions from bioethanol are regarded as part of nature's own carbon cycle.) This form of fuel wasn't new – the 1908 Model T Ford also had the capability to run on such a fuel – and FlexiFuel engines proved more popular in some countries than others, but these were part of Volvo's continuing drive to create more environmentally responsible cars.

Among the V70 models, the DRIVe was the budget version, and some people seemed put off by what would at first appear to be a hugely underpowered 1.6-litre turbo diesel. It was not a Volvo engine, but a PSA-BMW unit, that was used in a range of Peugeots, Fords and Minis. The towing capacity of the car with this engine was reduced by as much as 300kg. However, in both the V70 and the C30 (which also used this engine), performance is impressive given the low power. The

The V70 has always been a firm favourite with police forces – the fact that the new model had even more room was an added advantage.

Beach rescue: the 2007 California-inspired surf car concept.

suspension was lowered by 30mm and large tyres helped to cushion the bumpy ride.

The DRIVe V70 was also quite an interesting car for the Volvo estate timeline, because it challenged people's conceptions of a big Volvo being a gas guzzler: here was a Volvo estate that was capable of matching cheap hatchbacks for fuel economy, and a range of up to 1100 miles was claimed. In many ways, it was a clever idea, using cost-effective ideas to produce a car that would appeal to fleet users and individuals hit by company car tax rules throughout the EU, which targeted larger engines. The DRIVe was offered with four different levels of trim – being frugal didn't mean that you had to show it. You could spec your DRIVe to be as plush as any other V70 in the range.

The last V70s featured a smart instrument display, through which the driver could customise the style of the illumination and readings, whilst subtle interior lighting within door handles and trays made for an elegant touch. For countries that would need it, a heated steering wheel was an option.

As with other models in the range, the last V70s were equipped with Volvo's latest safety technology, including City Safety, which was introduced in 2006 and standardised across all new Volvos from 2008. Its main benefit was to reduce the incidence of whiplash and other neck-related injuries caused by low-speed traffic accidents, but it had the added benefit of reducing accidental scrapes.

Given the constraints due to the marque's ownership at the time, the

Half of XC70 production went to the mighty North American market. In 2014 Swedish footballer Zlatan Ibrahimovic featured in an advertising campaign with the XC70.

The 2012 face-lift had chrome inserts, revised interior fittings, new wheels, a softer cabin and Volvo's Sensus infotainment system.

V70 P3 was probably as good as it ever could have been – towards the end of its production, at least.

On 25 April 2016 a bright red Volvo V70 drove off the Gothenburg production line and into the Volvo Museum collection. This was the last ever V70: production had come to an end. It was Sweden's best-selling car for over 20 years. It had grabbed the world's attention and challenged opinions, turning countless people into loyal Volvo customers. Across three generations, 1,636,647 V70s had been distributed throughout the world.

V70 P3 Production 2011-2016: 333,164.

The end of an era: the very last V70 enters the Volvo Museum on the April 25, 2016.

Refreshed cabin of the last of the 2016 V70.

15 V60

In 2011, the replacement for the V50 went on sale, and continues as part of the Volvo line-up at the time of writing. It was very much like its predecessor: a European car. The design brief was to make the compact estate car seem more coupé and sports-like than ever. It was not intended to compete with the traditional estate car – for the customer wanting lots of cargo space, there was the V70 or XC70. Instead, its compact style, with wedge shape and sloping roofline screamed sports car. Its sculpted bonnet, small rear windows, and short overhangs emphasised the point. Sleek and pleasing, the V60 is a very easy car to live with. It is aimed at younger motorists who might not normally think of buying an estate car. The slanted rear tailgate echoes that of the P1800 ES sports wagon.

The V60 was equipped with a whole range of new Volvo safety measures, including pedestrian detection, Driver Alert Control (DAC), Lane Departure Warning (LDW), Blind Spot Information System (BLIS) and articulated headlights.

Two petrol and three diesel engine options were offered, ranging from the

D2, D3, and D4, as you may expect. The 150bhp T3 petrol engine returns 48.7mpg, whilst at the top of fuel economy in the diesel range is the D2 with a claimed figure of 76.3mpg. The world of the Volvo estate car had reached new levels of fuel economy. Many 240 owners of the '80s would find it difficult to believe that a new Volvo estate car would be capable of such figures. A D5 plug-in

Volvo refers to the V60 as a sports wagon rather than an estate. Its plan was to make it feel more 'coupé' than 'estate.'

Cargo area of the V60.

hybrid version was added in 2013. This diesel/electric car features an electric motor as part of the rear subframe assembly, which produces up to 70hp. As with start technology found on many cars today, the engine cuts out when it's not required, making a reduction in both emissions and fuel consumption, with the latter potentially increasing to 124mpg! As you would expect, for all this innovation, the car has a high price, as do similar offerings from other manufacturers.

Polestar, Volvo's in-house sports tuning division, enhanced the V60 in 2014 with a version heavily influenced by racing themes. This was the first time that the relatively new enterprise had injected something into the mainstream market: the Polestar V60, appropriately named the 850 R Rebel Blue. Volvo, keen to regain some of that lost racing pedigree, now had a subdivision of specialist race professionals who could soup up the brand. In this case, the car began life as a V60 T6 R-Design, with all options included. Then it received the Polestar magic: 346bhp, faster gear changes, six-piston Brembo calipers, 20in custom wheels – not to mention Öhlins racing shock absorbers. For just under £50,000, it's on a par with the XC90, yet a totally different animal: a very rare car, and one that has put Volvo back on the map that the Rs vacated.

V60 Production 2011-March 2017: 327,744.

The sporty interior of the V60: at its best, the car can achieve 76mpg.

V60 Polestar: Volvo racing driver, Jan Nilsson, founded the Polstar company in 1996. 'Polestar engineered optimisation' reunites Volvo with high performance.

345bhp and 0–60 in 5.3 seconds, the V60 Polestar features a 3.0-litre straight six engine.

If an XC70 was too much, the V60 Cross Country filled the gap.

16 XC60

Back in 2007, at the North American Auto Show, Volvo unveiled a new crossover 4x4 concept car, a smaller version of the XC90. The new car was targeted at the BMW X3 and Freelander market. In fact, the Land Rover Freelander shared much of its platform with the new Volvo, a hangover from the days of Ford, although the XC60, as it was to be called, was miles ahead of its rivals, both in style and quality.

The concept car not only offered the world a preview of the XC60; it was full of design innovations and showcased Volvo's new 'DNA' which was to permeate throughout its range over the years. As Volvo Cars Design Director, Steve Mattin, put it, "With more expressive, emotive shapes, it will be a magnet for the viewer's eyes. If you say that you recognise a Volvo

224 KW AND 0-100 KM/H IN 7.3 SECS. THAT'S ONE HELL OF A SIX PACK.

THE VOLVO XC60 T6

Volvo. for life

The crossover XC60 has been a global success.

A crash test at 35mph demonstrates the structural strength of the car - opening the doors would not be a problem after a head-on collision at this speed.

Interior of the XC60 – a very pleasant place to be.

from 50 metres today, I want to get to the point where you will instantly spot it from twice that distance in the future."

The XC60 concept was hardly changed at all when it entered production the following year. It was the first to feature the revised new Volvo badge, and the distinctive face of the new generation of Volvo cars.

A wide variety of engines and options were available from the word go, whilst the plug-in hybrid went on sale in 2012 in the US, probably with an eye on California (always an environmental champion) and what the car could do there. Awareness of the environmental impact of motoring is increasing, and while combining a 4x4 with fuel economy is not a common objective, with the XC60 forward-thinking Volvo demonstrated what is possible. More conventional power plants offered ranged from a 2.0-litre petrol to the T6 AWD and, in diesel, form the range went from D3 as used in the S40/V60 to the D5.

A slight update was added in 2014, eliminating black trim and adding more chrome touches. Inside, a larger touch-screen control panel and further interior options gave more refinement. The XC60 is a very satisfying car to live with. For those wanting a little more than a cross country estate while not as flamboyant as the range-topping XC90, this car fits the bill. With the right engine choice, a 130mph top speed was quoted. A sporty-looking medium-size 4x4 in most cases would spend as much time off-road as any XC90.

Volvo's marketing of the XC60 was strongly aimed at the younger professional. In 2016, its new advertising campaign celebrated the multicultural nature of its growing workforce, featuring

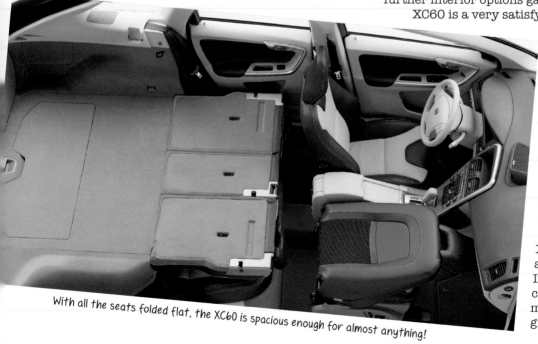

With all the seats folded flat, the XC60 is spacious enough for almost anything!

2016 Model XC60.

Volvo employees across the company in many different roles – from designers and engineers to workers on the factory floor. Björn Annwall, Senior Vice President, Marketing Sales and Service at Volvo Cars summed up the company's campaign: "At the moment we have close to 50 nationalities actively contributing to the design, development, marketing, sales and service of our cars ... We believe that a large part of Volvo's continuing success can be attributed to diversity and what we call the 'Volvo spirit.'"

The band Swedish House Mafia featured in one of the Volvo marketing films aimed at the younger demographic.

The XC60 has done Volvo proud: it has become its biggest seller in the current range. A crossover between an SUV and estate car, it still offers the defining ingredients of a Volvo estate and is a significant player in a segment where buyers wouldn't naturally consider owning a traditional estate car.

The XC60 Production 2008-March 2017: 859,488.

'Made by Sweden' – an advertising campaign that reflected Volvo's pride in, and appreciation of, its diverse workforce.

In 2013, Volvo teamed up with dance band Swedish House Mafia for a marketing campaign for the XC60.

17 XC90 Second Generation

Volvo's new flagship XC90 was introduced for model year 2015. The first 1927 cars (referencing the year Volvo was founded) were available only by special internet order. They were individually numbered and specially badged – the very first was bought by the King of Sweden. Like its predecessor,

The 2014 XC90 has proved extremely popular in the North American market.

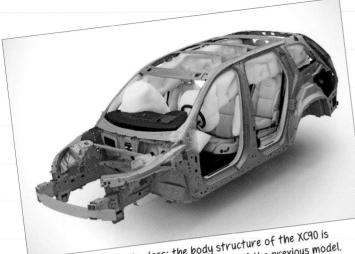

Safest car in its class: the body structure of the XC90 is stronger, lighter and larger than that of the previous model.

At the heart of the interior: the Sensus infotainment system.

Volvo's new flagship car was marketed heavily towards a US audience.

The US market had changed significantly since the launch of the first generation XC90 in 2004. Then the market segment had little competition but, as the old XC90 sales fell, Volvo had to do so much more than just produce an upgraded SUV. The Audi Q7, BMW X5, Mercedes ML, Lexus GX, Jaguar F-Pace, Acura MDX, and even the Land Rover Discovery are all options for potential Volvo customers, so Volvo's new car took them all on.

Longer, wider and lower than its predecessor, it contained the very latest of Volvo's safety features, including Active Bending Lights (ABL) and Active High Beams (AHB), blind spot detection, City Safety collision avoidance, collision detection and auto-braking, distance alert, lane departure warning, and rear-collision warning. How far safety has come since Volvo introduced the seat belt in 1959.

It is a sign of how far engines have come that the XC90 has a 2.0-litre engine. Even 10 years ago, that would have seemed hugely underpowered, but don't let it deceive you. The new car is both turbocharged and supercharged, delivering 316hp through an eight-speed automatic gearbox. The hybrid models also feature a 80hp electric motor.

Volvo's Drive-E engines are available throughout the range. In the XC90 the T8 twin engine plug-in hybrid accelerates from 0-62 in 5.9 seconds, impressive for a mainstream SUV that weighs over 2.3 tons.

The press loved it, and so did the public. It might look huge from the outside, but inside it was driver heaven. It had a simplified dashboard, and Sensus technology (Volvo's pioneering approach to intuitive convenience which includes the ability to lock or unlock your car via a smart-phone app).

Designed for ultimate ease and comfort, it was also incredibly quiet, "... a driving experience so noiseless I could be in space," as *Guardian* journalist Zoe Williams put it.

Side-impact crash testing.

For roll-over testing, the car is launched sideways.

This test was conducted by the US organisation Insurance Institute for Highway Safety as an overlap impact. The XC90 had one of the best results in its class.

The XC90 saw Volvo change its image once again. Volvo called the new campaign "a New Beginning." A collaboration with Swedish artist/producer Avicii in 2015 featuring a reworking of the classic song *Feeling Good*, and personal reflections by Avicii that echoed Volvo's process of re-evaluation and renewal, and was clearly aimed at Volvo's younger market.

The tag line 'Made By Sweden' was adopted, reinforcing Volvo's ethos. As Volvo puts it: "In Sweden, care for people is a priority. Everyone is important – all life is important – and that has always carried through naturally into Volvo's ethos of car making. It's this care for the wellbeing of driver, passengers and everyone around the car that has always defined Volvo. And always will."

After several years of intense investment and from listening to its customers, Volvo said, it had refined its brand. "The result is a new, more nimble and customer-responsive Volvo Cars," said Alain Visser, Senior Vice President Sales, Marketing & Customer Service at Volvo Car Group.

With the new beginning, came a new look –shown most clearly by its new T-shaped 'Thor's Hammer' running lights. "Anyone who looks in their rear-view mirror is going to know immediately that there is a new XC90 behind them," said Thomas Ingenlath, senior vice president of design – and these new lights clearly have the potential to become as iconic a part of Volvo's design as the company logo, or vertical tailgate.

A new dynamic has been kick-started by the second generation XC90. Just as the 850 reinvented the brand in the '90s, Volvo has moved once again into the spotlight.

The XC90 is still in production at the time of printing. 2015-March 2017: 151,313.

Protection for all inside: the XC90 could be a life saver.

A new beginning: for the launch of the XC90 in 2015, Volvo collaborated with Swedish DJ Avicii – his reworking of the Nina Simone classic, Feeling Good, featured in the campaign.

2017 XC90 Excellence: a special edition first class SUV. With just four seats instead of seven, it oozed luxury. It had wide individual reclining rear seats, a retractable control touchscreen, Champagne fridge, a heating/cooling cup holder, and handmade crystal glasses, mood lighting and foldaway tables, and was powered by the 400hp T8 hybrid engine.

18 V90

Made for a new world. 60 years of estate car production has led Volvo to this all-important car. This is the Volvo estate everyone has been waiting for, the combination of luxurious Scandinavian refinement and high speed technology encapsulated in the most sophisticated Volvo estate car to date.

Introduced in 2016 to replace the V70, alongside its saloon variant (the S90), the V90 is essentially the

2016 V90: the most luxurious and technologically focused Volvo estate car to date.

Over 60 years of Volvo estate design culminated in this car. An additional 1000 engineers were employed to work on the SPA platform.

The XC90 cabin shows the Volvo signature – what a comfortable place to be!

estate version of the hip XC90 SUV. At first glance, the most apparent change in design from traditional Volvo estates is the lack of a vertical tailgate, which will be a disappointment to some. The V90 looks more like its German rivals, but it's a Volvo through-and-through, with safety and comfort at its heart.

Volvo has an ambitious plan for 2020: "Our vision is that by 2020 no one should be killed or seriously injured in a new Volvo car," Håkan Samuelsson, President and CEO, Volvo Cars.

That is quite a wish, but there is every chance that Volvo will achieve it. Its IntelliSafe on-board computer systems is well on the way to doing so: pedestrian detection, forward and rear collision warning, lane keeping aid, park assist, radar, active high beam, road sign information, driver alert control, and roll stability control are just some of the features packed into the V90. The list is long, and, like most new cars, the options can feel bewildering. Needless to say, this is the way of the future.

The V90 is the pinnacle of Volvo's achievements, from the SPA platform to the design of the plush interior. Automotive computer designers are today as much if not more important than those that design the power-plants.

Gothenburg is very excited about its latest estate car, and with good reason. The new V90 is a thing of

beauty and innovation. As with the XC90, the V90 and S90 have the same 'Thor's Hammer' headlight system. At 2300kg, it is not a light car, but the performance figures are reasonable.

The fastest T5 version has 254hp, but just wait for the hot Polestar version if you want to see something exciting – perhaps it will be as exciting as the S60 R or 850 T5?

It is planned that the V90 will continue in production for many years, showcasing the very best of Volvo, with an elegant touch screen display, wraparound console, and plenty of legroom in the rear. The car's lineage is clear – its graceful lines and sporty curves as much a part of popular car culture as it is a part of our own lives.

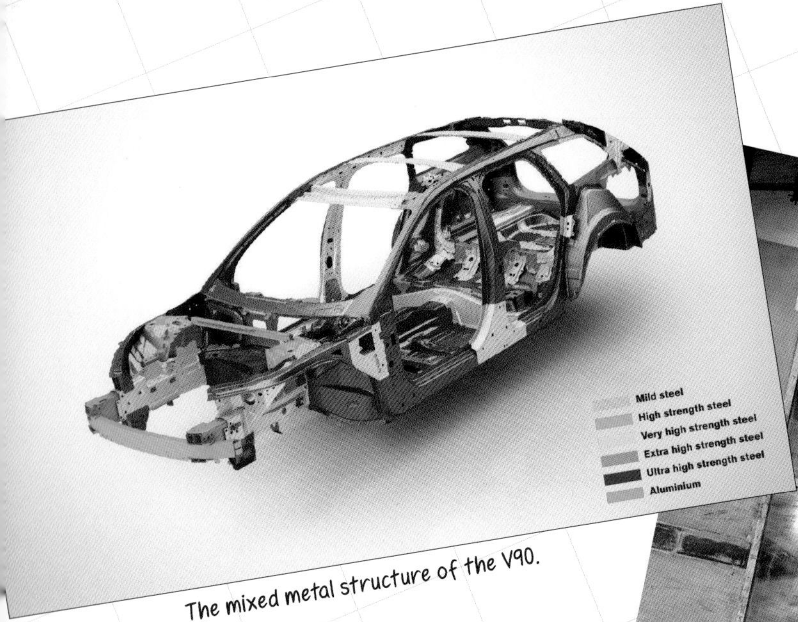

The Volvo estate car – design icon and faithful companion

Mild steel
High strength steel
Very high strength steel
Extra high strength steel
Ultra high strength steel
Aluminium

The mixed metal structure of the V90.

Side impact testing of the V90 at the Volvo Safety Centre. Volvo has made a monumental public promise: no occupant of a new Volvo car will be killed or seriously injured by 2020.

The first line of V90 production at Gothenburg in June 2016.

2017 V90 Cross Country. Now somewhere between the XC and V90, the off-road estate car is the most efficient: up to 134mpg, powered by the T8 hybrid engine.

The Swedish police force was naturally first to adopt the new V90.

The modern Volvo estate is one of the most versatile cars in the world, appealing to the adventurer, city commuter, business executive, artist, technician, jack-of-all-trades and family, but most of all it is a car for real people.

It is very hard today to build a safe car that gives the raw driving experience of twenty years ago or more, but that has never been Volvo's main focus. If you want stupid performance then it is probably best to buy a different brand. The Volvo will always be a Volvo. One thing is certain: the V90 is as safe and comfortable a place as you could wish to be.

The V90 is still in production at the time of printing.

19 The future

From the first ÖV4 saloon to the current V90, the Volvo estate is a motoring icon that just gets better over time. It went from being unknown, to the butt of the jokes, to the car you aspire to own.

Volvo has always been at the forefront of automotive safety, striving to make cars safer both for their occupants, and the world at large, as evidenced by the decision to give away the technology for three-point safety belt harness to encourage other automakers to install them, to IntelliSafe. Such safety measures advance, year by year, and the marque is rightly recognised the world over as a pioneer and leader in this area. Volvo's safety technology has saved countless lives, and often other marques have followed where

60 years of Volvo estate production.

Volvo leads. Driverless cars already feature many of these elements, and Volvo will undoubtedly continue to offer significant safety contributions to this emerging car segment.

Volvo is one of the most environmentally conscious vehicle manufacturers in the world. All European Volvo factories are now powered entirely by renewable energy. Electric cars are at the centre of Volvo's future planning. It intends to have a fully electric vehicle on sale by 2020. The existing T8 hybrid engine is the first step in this ambitious plan. A smaller SPA system for a new 40 series of production vehicles will feature a new technology sharing platform. It plans on selling one million hybrid cars by 2025.

So what will the future Volvo estate be like? Will it be self driving? More than likely it will be capable of such things, but it will also undoubtedly look and feel everything that we have come to identify as a Volvo estate car. One thing is for sure, Volvo is not going to forget the car that put it on the road to success: as long as the Swedish manufacturer is in business, there will always be a new Volvo estate.

Made by Sweden

Volvo estate car timeline

Decade						
1950s	Duett 1953-69	Amazon 1956-70				
1960s	Duett 1953-69	Amazon 1956-70	145 1966-74			
1970s	Amazon 1956-70	145 1966-74	P1800 ES 1972-73	245/265 1974-93		
1980s	245/265 1974-93	740/760 1982-92				
1990s	245/265 1974-93	740/760 1982-92	960 1990-98	850 1991-96	V40 1995-2004	V70 Classic 1996-2000	V70 P2 1999-2007
2000s	V40 1995-2004	V70 Classic 1996-2000	V70 P2 1999-2007	XC90 2001-2014	V50 2003-2011	V70 P3 2007-2016	XC60 2008-present
2010s	XC90 2001-2014	V50 2003-2011	V70 P3 2007-2016	XC60 2008-present	V60 2011-2017	XC90 2nd Generation 2014-2016	V90 2016-present

Links

Volvo Club of Sweden
Includes links to Volvo clubs around the world.
www.svis.se

Volvo Club UK
Around since 1962, this is a great source of information on any and every Volvo car. Includes Volvo press releases and brochures, and a wealth of technical specifications among its resources, as well as interesting articles on all things Volvo. Also home of the Volvo High Mileage Club – read stories from real Volvo owners who have pushed their Volvos (and their odometers) to the limits!
www.volvoclub.org.uk

Volvo Enthusiasts' Club UK
The only club specifically dedicated to the classic Volvo. Lots of information and local meetings.
www.volvoenthusiastsclub.co.uk

Volvo Club of America
Volunteer organization, run by and for Volvo owners, enthusiasts, collectors, restorers and all others who wish to experience and enjoy the fellowship, resources, activities, purchase discounts (new Volvos, parts, service, exclusive merchandise) related to Volvo cars, past, present and future.
www.vcoa.org

Swedespeed
A great online community for Volvo owners and enthusiasts.
www.swedespeed.com

The Washington Volvo Club
Founded in 1975, the Washington Volvo Club is the continuation of a club begun in 1958, and has become a truly international Volvo community.
www.meetup.com/volvoclubdc/

Canadian Volvo Club
The Club's goal is to promote enthusiasm for Volvo cars. All Volvo models are welcome and citizens from all countries can join.
www. canadianvolvoclub.org

Australia
Various clubs online, including Volvo Car Club of NSW www. volvocarclubnsw.com and Volvo Car Club of Victoria www. volvovic.org.au

Also from Veloce Publishing –

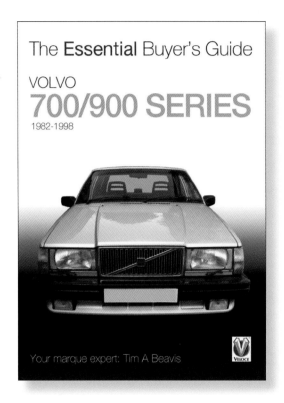

The **Essential** Buyer's Guide

VOLVO
700/900 SERIES
1982-1998

Your marque expert: Tim A Beavis

Having this book in your pocket is just like having a real marque expert at your side. Benefit from Tim Beavis' years of Volvo experience, learn how to spot a bad car quickly, and how to assess a promising one like a true professional. Get the right car at the right price!

ISBN: 978-1-845844-56-1
Paperback • 19.5x13.9cm • 64 pages • 100 colour pictures

For more information and price details, visit our website at www.veloce.co.uk • email: info@veloce.co.uk
• Tel: +44(0)1305 260068

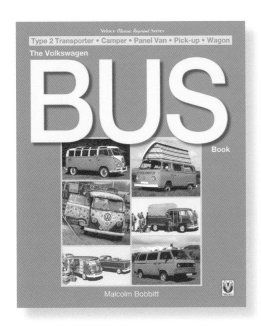

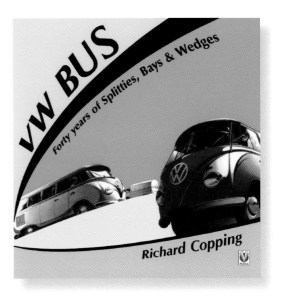

Available again after a long absence!
The story of VW's Transporter, Bus and Camper,
from origins to the present day, and why it's one
of the world's most familiar vehicles.

ISBN: 978-1-845849-95-5
Paperback • 25x20.7cm • 208 pages
• 258 colour and b&w pictures

A methodical, yet lively record of VW's
iconic Transporter over its first 40-years.
Model history and range development,
specifications,performance, plus marketing
and advertising strategies are all discussed and
stylishly illustrated with period photographs.

ISBN: 978-1-787111-23-3
Paperback • 22.5x22.5cm • 176 pages
• 181 pictures

For more information and price details, visit our website at www.veloce.co.uk • email: info@veloce.co.uk
• Tel: +44(0)1305 260068

Why not check out our other imprint, Hubble and Hattie?

Helpful advice on how to get the most out of car journeys with your canine companion – whether travelling for five minutes or five hours. Packed with original colour photographs, plus information from expert veterinarians.

ISBN: 978-1-845843-79-3
Paperback • 21x14.8cm • 80 pages
• 90 colour pictures

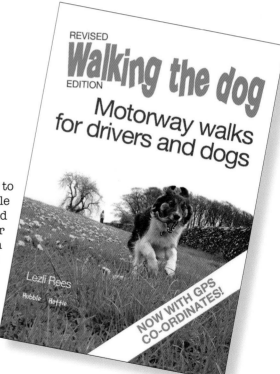

All motorway drivers will benefit from this guide to walks within 5 miles of motorway exits. The whole of the UK is covered, from Exeter to Perth and Swansea to Canterbury. Use this book to discover countryside walks for drivers, dogs, and families, with recommended activities and suitable places to eat along the way.

ISBN: 978-1-845848-86-6
Paperback • 15x10.5cm • 208 pages
• 200 colour pictures

For more information and price details, visit our website at www.veloce.co.uk • email: info@veloce.co.uk • Tel: +44(0)1305 260068

Also from Hubble and Hattie –

For more information and price details, visit our website at www.veloce.co.uk • email: info@veloce.co.uk
• Tel: +44(0)1305 260068

Index